Practical Car Restoration

Practical Car Restoration

A Guidebook with Lessons from a 1930 Franklin Rebuild

CHARLES R. WILMARTH III

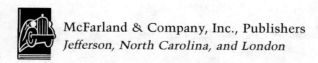

McFarland & Company, Inc., Publishers
Jefferson, North Carolina, and London

LIBRARY OF CONGRESS CATALOGUING-IN-PUBLICATION DATA

Wilmarth, Charles R., 1939–
    Practical car restoration : a guidebook with lessons from a 1930
Franklin rebuild / Charles R. Wilmarth III.
        p.   cm.
    Includes bibliographical references and index.

    ISBN-13: 978-0-7864-2511-2
    ISBN-10: 0-7864-2511-3 (softcover : 50# alkaline paper) ∞

    1. Antique and classic cars — Conservation and restoration —
Amateurs' manuals.   2. Franklin automobile — Conservation and
restoration — Amateurs' manuals.   I. Title
TL152.2.W55   2006
629.28'72 — dc22   2006020494

British Library cataloguing data are available

On the cover: The author's 1930 Franklin, before and after restoration.

Manufactured in the United States of America

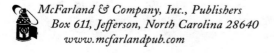

McFarland & Company, Inc., Publishers
    Box 611, Jefferson, North Carolina 28640
        www.mcfarlandpub.com

Table of Contents

Preface

I grew up in Northern Idaho in the late 1940s and early 1950s. In that time and place everyone drove old cars — not for reasons of nostalgia, but because it was all that they could afford.

Most of the cars in the area were late 1920 or 1930 models. They were old even then and required a lot of maintenance. Another problem was that the people working on them didn't really understand what they were doing. It was not unlike today: the young people understood all the gadgets and the older people didn't. This also was an era when haywire (baling wire) was a common repair item. A soup can worked as a hubcap, a nail was used for a cotter pin and everyone used reliners in their tires.

From an early age I had mechanical aptitude — one of my favorite toys was an old alarm clock that I used to take apart and reassemble after changing the gears around. I learned a lot by observing people working on their cars, and by the time I was twelve years old, I got to help. Then, when I was old enough to drive, I began working on my own cars. I overhauled the engine in my 1949 Plymouth at seventeen. After I completed high school, I joined the Navy and worked as an aircraft mechanic for four years. After my discharge, I worked on heavy equipment and trucks most of my working years.

I restored my first car while still in the Navy. And all through my working years, I had several old cars to play with and to repair. After I moved to Arizona, my neighbor and I restored my 1928 Dodge for the Great American Race. Later we restored his 1930

Marmon coupe. I was making furniture at the time and so I had plenty of woodworking tools to do the body wood in the Marmon. I liked the woodwork so well that I wanted to do another wood-bodied car.

A 1930 Franklin gave me the challenge I was looking for. It was a bigger car to fit my size and one that needed almost all of the wood replaced. I decided to record the process in pictures and words. That was the beginning of this book. Later, I expanded the book to cover the process of finding a car, learning about it and using it after the restoration.

I knew from the start that this was a very narrow field. There wouldn't be many people restoring 1930 Franklins, or any Franklin of this era, so I attempted to broaden the scope of this book to cover cars of the classic era. In doing this, though, I have had to be more general in my descriptions. Where I am specific in detail, I point out how you might take the technique that I used and apply it to your own situation. My goal is to show that anyone with the desire can restore a car.

Some restoration books, I feel, intimidate the restorer by telling the reader to take the engine to a shop to be rebuilt, to have a professional shop paint the car and do the upholstery, and so on. You end up not being a car restorer, but a general contractor just overseeing the project. You may or may not get a better restoration this way, but for sure it will cost you at least three times the amount of money you would spend doing most of the work yourself.

Yes, you will have to send some of the work out, unless you have access to an unusual amount of tools and equipment. But I will try to help you see where you can minimize the amount of work done by others.

I had a metal shop make the running boards and gas tank for my Franklin because I didn't have the equipment to form the metal. The chrome plating I also sent out. An artist friend painted the wood grain on the dash and window frames, and another artist did the pinstriping. All of the rest of the work I did myself—and if I can do it, anyone can. I didn't attempt to make a 100-point show car

2

either, which would have added to the cost considerably. I think that it is safe to say that any car that has been restored isn't an original anyway. The real issue is, how close do you get?

My idea is to restore the car to preserve it as much as possible in its original state, but still have a car that is drivable and safe for today's traffic. The Road Rally Rules are a good guideline to follow.

After my Franklin was restored, I wasn't satisfied with some aspects of the job, so I made changes to correct the problems. This will happen more often than not if you are restoring the car to drive.

I expanded the book to include some suggestions for getting involved in the old car hobby. For most people this wouldn't be necessary, but for those of us that hang around the shop by ourselves too much, getting involved in the social aspect of the hobby is an important and sometimes difficult step.

Another interesting part of the hobby is learning the history of the car company. In my case it was the Franklin Automobile Company and the H.H. Franklin Car Club. The history, in part, should at least be studied as part of the restoration process. Among other things, this will help you determine if any incorrect parts have been added to your car.

I have included some chapters on driving the car after the restoration. If you have restored the car for driving, then you will picture in your mind using it to take road trips. In this book I write about one trip that my wife and I took where I showed the car to hundreds of people. Having your car on the road like this gives you pride in the fact that you restored it with a certain amount of dependability.

That is why I started my hobby over fifty years ago — working to "keep them running." After all, cars were made to drive.

CHAPTER 1

Getting Started

To restore a car is a major undertaking, but certainly not an impossible task. I have heard of people taking up to fourteen years. The time required will vary as to the age, condition, make and model of the car. The time, tools and money that one has are also factors. How much of the work you do yourself and how much you farm out has to be considered. I have restored several cars and do most of the work myself and it takes me around five or six months, with help. I probably have more free time than most working people, but my time was not used exclusively in the restoration projects.

I am bringing up the time that car restoration takes to caution you that a lot of hours will be involved. I see ads all the time: "Car for sale, restoration started," or "Restoration 60%–70% completed." I have learned at an early age that not to finish a task is a waste of time and money. A project 75 percent finished will not bring 75 percent of its finished value. If you only have a few hours a week to work on the car, restoration will take so long that you will probably lose interest and be one of those people who sell their car before the job is complete. People with limited time, but with the desire to restore a car, should consider buying one that is over half completed. Usually the car can be purchased for less than the owner has in it. Maybe the job has just taken too long and the owner has lost interest, or maybe his wife wants the mess out of the garage so she can put her car back in it.

Speaking of wives: Is your spouse supportive of the project? I just read an ad: "Wife says either she or the car must go." It is tough to concentrate on the car with a spouse nagging about you spending so much time with it. It is far better when you both are interested and you can share in the pride of owning and driving a car that you restored. I would suggest if your spouse is overtly opposed to the project, it would be best not to undertake it. If she is as dead set against it as you are for it, unhappiness lies ahead.

The next thing you need is a place to work on the car. It seems to take about four times as much space to work on a car as it does to park it. You can get by with a two-car garage if you stack the parts outside and bring them in as needed. I will cover the step-by-step procedure later, but you will be ahead of the game if you have plenty of room to work around all sides of the car.

Now you may have reached the point where you are saying, "I can do this and it will be a lot of fun!" You are right on both counts. You could spend your time at the ball game, playing golf, watching TV, and so on. Nothing wrong with these activities, but when they are over, you have nothing to show for your time. I like to look back on each day and see what I have accomplished. Remember you are not killing time; time is killing you, so it is best to use it in a fruitful experience. If you still want to tackle a restoration project, go for it. The graveyard is full of people who were going to do something but never got around to it.

Okay: you are about ready to go for it; you have figured out the time, support, place to work, and you have the desire. One detail missing — the car. "What kind of car should I get?" That, of course, is up to the individual. This decision should be based on the car that you would like to have and what you plan to do with it. Some car rallies limit the cars to pre–World War II vintage or to a particular make. Most car clubs have tours, so if there is a club in your area you might check and see if they have specifications as to year, make and model.

What era of car do you like? Some people like the brass era (pre–1915). These cars are really attention-getters and great for tours in the summer as they are almost exclusively open cars, but they are not recommended for Minnesota in January. I like cars of the late 1920s and early 1930s. If this is your first restoration and you like this era, a Model-A Ford would be a good choice. They hold their value, parts are readily available, and they are easy to work on. A more drivable choice would be the early V8 Ford. If you want to stay away from a lot of body wood and have a car with parts that are fairly obtainable, a Dodge is worth considering. The bigger luxury cars of that era are great, but more expensive to buy; this would include makes such as Packard, Pierce, Chrysler and Cadillac. Hudson, Nash and Studebaker are good cars from the same era that sell considerably cheaper. Some people like a car that brings back memories: the first car that they owned, or the kind that they had when they got married. If we get into the 1950s era, the 1955 to 1957 Chevy will always be popular; the 1960s era had the Ford Mustang and the 1960s and 1970s had the muscle cars.

In this book I will show how I restored a 1930 Franklin. Some details won't apply to other makes, but the book will give you an idea of the step-by-step procedure that should be followed in any restoration. For example, if you remove the body, go through the chassis and running gear before replacing. If you plan to reupholster, painting the car first saves a lot of masking and eliminates the risk of paint on the upholstery. Going step by step will make the job easier. Obviously, though, you can skip chapters in this book that don't apply to your restoration. If your car has no body wood, skip that part. If you are not doing a complete restoration, you don't have to remove and replace the body; skip that part. Just remember, whatever you do, do it step by step.

By now, you should know what kind of car that you want — not necessarily the year, make and model, but the era and body style. I would like to have a roadster, but being six-foot-four, I am too big to get into most of them, so I opt for something roomier. Generally, cars are of decreasing value for the style of a given make and model in this order: Roadsters are the most valuable, then touring cars, coupés, 2-door sedans and finally 4-door sedans. These categories refer to the body styles and there are variations within each of them, but the list roughly covers them. For example, my Franklin is a 4-door club sedan, which means it has a five-window body as compared to a 4-door sedan which has seven windows. There is a great value difference on some makes, but for the majority, other factors may make more of a difference.

Restoring a car could be a good investment if you have a high-value car and the restoration job is good. For most restorations, however, the value lies in the process, the satisfaction, and the pride of accomplishment. If you get the money back that you put into the project, you are doing well. I see examples of this at every car auction that I attend. One case, to make a point, was a 1926 Hupmobile, a low-mileage original 4-door sedan that sold for less than it would cost to restore a good car to the same condition.

Finding the car you've decided you want is the next challenge. You may know someone who knows where some old cars are. I have heard stories of people finding a car in an old barn or shed. I came close to getting a couple of cars this way, but for most of us, buying through an ad is your best hope. Check your local or nearby city newspaper under antique and classic cars. If you find one this way, you won't have to travel so far to get it. The best place is *Hemmings Motor News*—as they say, it is the bible of the old car hobby. I would suggest subscribing for a year at least, and watching for the type and make of car you would like to have. There are also some weekly publications like *Old Car Weekly* that have ads in them. If you know what make of car you desire, you can join a club dedicated to it. Most of these clubs have newsletters with ads and are a great source for parts for their make. They are also a great help in obtaining technical information.

Old car auctions and swap meets are a good place to buy a car as you and the seller can look the car over and discuss it face to face.

It has been my experience that people in the hobby are generally pretty fair, honest and helpful. When you spot an ad for a car of interest to you and call about it, you can usually get a fair description. Keep in mind that if the seller says it is 100 percent completed, it may still have a few small parts missing. Unless you are buying from a professional dealer, the grading system used to rate a car's condition doesn't mean much. With this system cars are graded from 1 (which is like new) to 5 which is a real challenge to restore.

When I called about this Franklin, the seller described it fairly well. On the scale of 1 to 5, I pictured in my mind about a number 6 — a parts car. The seller told me the wood was bad, but all the parts were there except the headlights. Not knowing if headlights would be difficult to find, I located a set before I agreed to take the car.

After you and the seller have discussed the car and a ballpark price, the next thing is to go look at it. This is where it is not only convenient, but practical, to find a car as close to home as possible. You don't want to travel from coast to coast just to look at a car, especially one of low value. You might go around the world for a Duesenberg, but not for a 1949 Studebaker. Remember, you are looking for a car to restore, not one that is in mint condition.

What to look for when buying a car is the next important step. Check to see how many parts are missing or how many incorrect parts have been used in the car. Look also for clues to see if the car has been wrecked such as a bent frame or a lot of filler in the body. The instruments — such as clocks and gauges — are important items to have as there are so many changes within a given model for the same year that they may be difficult to replace. Don't be concerned with broken or missing glass unless it is curved glass. You will want to replace the flat glass in older cars anyway. Most mechanical parts can be found or replaced with modern parts. But do consider the replacement costs and factor that into the price.

Using the Franklin again as an example, the top wood and fabric material were missing. Had they been there but deteriorated to a point where they needed to be replaced, the value wouldn't have changed much but the car overall may have looked better. The only advantage to having the deteriorated parts in place would have been in making a pattern for the wood.

In conclusion, look for a car that is straight, with little rust and with most of its parts. Don't be too concerned with a bad top (fabric tops), worn upholstery, broken flat glass or deteriorated rubber, including the tires, as you will replace these things anyway. Obviously, the car will be repainted so the paint can also be disregarded.

Now we have covered the process from the desire to restore a car to actually buying one. Once you have your car, transport it to where you are going to work on it and then take an inventory of parts that you will need. Things like door handles, bumper guards and so on you won't need for some time, but there can be a long lag time in acquiring some parts, so it is best to get started searching for them. If you find that the carburetor or wheel or something else is obviously missing, you will need to start your search for that part also. Internal parts like bearings and pistons, you won't be able to tell until you take the components apart.

Also, look for the things that need fixing. I noticed a leak around the oil drain plug in my Franklin. If I hadn't caught this, I would have put the pan back on the engine after overhauling it and still had the leak. By seeing this problem early on, I was able to fix it while I had the pan off and didn't have to remove it twice. (It looked like a crack around the plug boss. When I heated the area with a torch, the crack opened up and was easy to see.)

Now is the time to do some research on the make and model of your car. The next chapter covers a brief history of the Franklin Company as an example of information to be gleaned before starting your project. Not all of the information will be necessary for your particular restoration project, but I believe this knowledge can be useful to those of you who share my interest in restoring old cars, no matter what make.

CHAPTER 2

History of the Franklin Automobile

Once you have purchased your car, it is a good idea to do some research on its make and model. It is not necessary to educate yourself on the complete history of the company, as far as the restoration goes. But later when you are at the car shows the more that you know of the car and the company, the more that you can share with the visitors. If you have a relatively rare make of automobile, like the Franklin, most people will not have heard of it and so will ask a lot of questions.

A good source of information is a car club pertaining to your make of car. Some clubs cover just one era of the make. I belong to the Dodge Brothers Club that covers Dodge cars up to 1938. The cutoff was decided on because before 1938 the company was called Dodge Brothers. After 1938 the Brothers name was dropped and just Dodge has been used up to the present time. Some clubs just deal with a model, like the Mustang or Corvette. This makes sense, as the owners are interested in the model and not a complete history of Ford or Chevrolet.

Most clubs that deal in older makes of cars that are no longer produced will cover the complete history. In fact the H.H. Franklin Club* covers any air-cooled automobiles during the era they were

*www.franklincar.org. Information about the H.H. Franklin Club and the Franklin Museum can be found at this website.

made. Probably 99 percent of the cars in the club are Franklins, but if you show up in your Knox,* I am sure you will be welcome.

The Willys-Overland-Knight Registry welcomes all sleeve valve automobiles. This means not only do they represent the products of the Willys-Overland Company, but also any car with a Knight engine.

Automobile clubs can be found on the Internet by putting in the make and following the links. For computer users this may be the way to go. I subscribe to *Old Cars,* which is a weekly publication. Each year they print out all of the car club addresses and phone numbers of whom to contact.

Even in this age of computers and the Internet, I still prefer books as a source of information. An encyclopedia of automobiles will give you a very basic history of each make, plus some technical information. This is a good place to start. There are also pictures of most of the cars, except the really rare ones.

The bigger car clubs have a research library, which as a member, you can access. This is the route to go for more detailed information. Of course, you can use the public library if you have access to one. I have never lived where I had easy access to a public library large enough, but I started a collection of books on pre-war cars years ago. I have tried to get a book on every make of car. That is impossible, of course, but the search for used books is a lot of fun.

This should give you some ideas of how to start your research. Since, in this book, I am dealing with a Franklin, I will cover a brief history of the company and the cars. The best source of information about the Franklin is *The Franklin Automobile Company* by Sinclair Powell. This book covers the history of the company and a biography of the principle people involved and is still available.[†]

John Wilkinson, the man behind the Franklin, was one of the

Kimes, Beverly Rae, and Henry Austin Clark, Standard Catalog of American Cars, *2nd ed. (Krause Publications, 1989), 788. Knox made cars in Springfield, Massachusetts, from 1900 to 1914. Up to 1910 they made air-cooled models using pins protruding from the cylinders to dissipate the heat.*

†Sinclair Powell, The Franklin Automobile Company *(Society of Automotive Engineers, 1999).*

early automobile pioneers. Unlike some of the others that tinkered with the horseless carriage, he was educated as an engineer. He also came from a wealthy family, which is always an advantage. By 1900, he had a working automobile, but like other pioneers in the field, his first car wasn't perfect. In 1901, after some business misadventures with early partners, he approached Herbert H. Franklin. Franklin had a die casting business by this time and was well known for his business savvy. Wilkinson apparently had no problem naming the car after the company that was going to manufacture them. He had the job of chief engineer and received some stock in the company.

Wilkinson was an advocate of air-cooling. Whether his advocacy was the reason for his first cars having four cylinders or because air-cooling makes a car run smoother running, I can only speculate. In either case, it was good engineering practice, as four small cylinders will have a lot more cooling surface than one big cylinder of equal displacement.

Franklin cars, with John Wilkinson at the helm had three things in common: the air-cooled engine, full elliptic springs and wooden frames. These features were all part of the concept of lightweight and flexible design. Wilkinson was also a promoter of "form follows function," a concept which led to designs beyond conventional-looking automobiles.

The early Franklins, from 1902 through 1905, looked similar to other cars of the era, except the overall profile was lower. Other makes of cars with their one- or two-cylinder engines that had to be mounted under the seat had higher profiles.

Franklin mounted their four-cylinder engine crossways in the front of the car. This was to facilitate the cooling by the ram air effect. In 1906, Franklin had developed a six-cylinder engine. This engine was longer than the four-cylinder engine and was mounted lengthwise. The engine had a gear-driven fan in front to help the cooling. The cars from 1906 to 1910 had a round grill in front with a rounded hood. Due to the appearance, these cars were known as the barrel-hood models. They still looked similar to other cars of that era, though.

This is a good example of a cross engine Franklin on the left and a barrel-hood model on the right.

In 1911, Franklin came out with the Renault-style hood. The name derived from the French car with the radiator behind the engine. Of course, the Franklin didn't have a radiator, but the appearance was similar. Here, in my opinion, Franklin regressed in both design and engineering. The design may have been OK, but the appearance was getting too far from the conventional, and that always spells disaster for sales. On the engineering side, the cooling fan was built into the flywheel at the back of the engine. This meant that the air was pulled through the engine to cool it. It is common knowledge that it is more efficient to push air than to pull it. (I admit that I am looking at this with about ninety years of hindsight.) This is a good example of form following function. If the blower would have been placed in the front of the engine, by necessity the form would have been more conventional.

Here is a Renault style Franklin roadster. My guess is that it is a 1914 model.

The company was in the forefront in many engineering aspects. They used full elliptic springs, which essentially doubled the length of the springs. It was known then that the longer the spring, the better the ride. Of course, you would run into design limitations making a semi-elliptic spring twice as long. Franklin made use of full elliptic springs without any radius rods or sway bars. Aluminum pistons were incorporated in the 1915 models when a lot of other cars still used cast iron.

Franklins were designed to be lightweight. More importantly, the unsprung weight was kept to a minimum by the use of a tubular front axle and light alloy rear end housing. With these features, the Franklins got excellent gas and tire mileage. Another plus for the air-cooled engine was that you didn't have to worry about your engine

It was difficult to get good pictures of all of the cars but the second and fourth cars from the left are the horse-collar models.

freezing. (This was in the day before antifreeze.) I believe the reason such a high percentage of Franklins survive today is the fact that the engine didn't freeze up and crack the block, like it did in water-cooled cars. Water pump seals hadn't been developed with any degree of durability yet, so air-cooling eliminated that problem.

In 1921, the horse-collar model came out. The name refers to the shape of the grill molding. These were the homeliest cars that the company had yet produced. Even the dealers thought so and persuaded H. H. Franklin to produce a car that they could sell.

A designer by the name of Frank deCausse designed a conventional and quite handsome automobile. It had a "radiator" shell with a hood ornament on top. Wilkinson quit in protest. This new form didn't follow any function. I guess he didn't consider selling them a

This is a row of Frank deCausse era Franklins. Note the "radiator cap" on the car closest.

function, but a radiator cap must have been just too much for him to take.

By this time, a scirocco fan that was driven by the crankshaft was incorporated on the front of the engine. Finally, they became the cars they should have been years before. They had a good-looking design and a blower to push the air. John Wilkinson was a good engineer in my opinion, but he didn't change with the times. By 1925, a new generation of engineers had come on the scene and they were designing cars that appealed to the buying public. The Franklin Company was to build their best cars after Wilkinson left, but they were already behind the times.

By the mid-to-late 1920s, the more expensive cars were going to eight-cylinder engines. Even Hupmobile* had a straight-eight by 1924. The Franklins were still using a driveline brake in 1926 when less expensive cars had four-wheel brakes. Franklins also were underpowered for their time, but by 1928 they had almost doubled their horsepower from a few years earlier. In 1928, the wood frame gave way to a pressed steel one.

By 1930, when my Franklin was made, the company had come a long way since John Wilkinson had left. They had a new engine with removable aluminum cylinder heads. It had bigger valves for better breathing, aluminum connecting rods to cut down on the reciprocating weight and a counter-balanced crankshaft. By some accounts, it put out ninety-five horsepower. With four-wheel hydraulic brakes, it was comparable to other cars in its price range. The problems were that by 1930, other higher-priced cars had eight, twelve, or sixteen cylinders. Even mid-priced cars had eight cylinder engines. Franklin had fallen behind the curve and just couldn't catch up.

H. H. Franklin knew in 1929 that he had to increase production in order to increase profits. He borrowed five million dollars to increase the production and to add to the engineering budget. He was successful in increasing the production. In fact, in 1929 they almost doubled the number of cars produced. The problem was that they didn't sell as many as they produced. Sales were up for the 1929 season, but not enough to keep up with the production. This left a lot of unsold cars going into the 1930 season. Most automobile manufacturers had their best year in 1929. In fact, the sales of those companies that survived the depression didn't equal the 1929 sales until after World War II. Packard[†] had their best year ever in 1929, making a profit of twenty-eight million dollars.

*Bill Cuthbert, The Hupmobile Story (M.T. Publishing Company, 2004), 90. The straight eight engine was developed in 1924 for the 1925 model year.

[†]Beverly Rae Kimes, Packard: A History of the Motorcar and the Company (Princeton Publishing, 1978), 292. Several figures emerge describing the profits of the company in 1929. Some are rounded-off numbers that reflect the calendar year. Kimes gives the total of $25,912,000 for the fiscal year. No one disagrees that it was the best year for the company.

Here are several 1930 Franklins, except for the third one from the left that appears to be a 1932 model. Note the single bar bumper and lack of sun visor.

There was a depression in 1921 and 1922 during which several automobile manufacturers went out of business, but years before the stock market crash in October of 1929 that signaled the start of the Great Depression. Even though the late 1920s was a boom time, many more manufacturers ceased production. Dort,* though solvent, shut down in 1924. Hugh Chalmers† sold his automobile company, which later became part of Chrysler. Winton,§ the oldest manufacture

---

Kimes and Clark, Standard Catalog of American Cars, *2nd ed., 418. Dort made cars in Flint, Michigan, from 1915 to 1924.*

†*Kimes and Clark,* Standard Catalog, *2nd ed., 257. Chalmers made cars in Detroit from 1908 to 1924. Maxwell bought out Chalmers and then Chrysler took over the Maxwell-Chalmers Company to start Chrysler in 1924.*

§*Bernard J. Golias and Thomas F. Saal,* Famous but Forgotten *(Golias Publisher, 1997), 108. Winton did not make the first car in America, but was the first to manufacture them starting in 1897. The company shut down its Cleveland, Ohio, factory in 1924.*

of automobiles in the United States, went out of business. It was becoming a big business where the economy of numbers was what mattered.

One reason so many companies shut down was that the most expensive part of the car to build was the body. When Dodge Brothers* teamed up with the Edward Budd Company to stamp out car bodies, it spelled doom for small manufacturers. It took millions of dollars to buy the giant presses and make the dies to stamp out a car body. The cost is quickly recovered if you make at least one hundred thousand cars, but a company like Franklin with around eight thousand cars made a year couldn't compete.

Franklin didn't have a press big enough to stamp out a fender. The front fenders on my 1930 were made in two pieces and seamed together. The body on my Dodge Brothers Victory Six was stamped out with four pieces of metal. The economy of scale played the pivotal role in the demise of many automobile manufacturers.

The only hope a small company like Franklin had to survive was to make high-end automobiles where the profit margin was higher. A custom department was established with the top-of-the-line coachwork. From the perspective of the Franklin Company, this was a step in the right direction. The most beautiful Franklins ever were made during this period.

No one could foresee the length and depth of the Great Depression. Franklin had survived the 1921–1922 depression and if they were like a lot of the other automobile companies, they could hold on a year or two until things would work out. One way to hold on to the company was to make a better car for less money.

Most auto historians agreed that 1932 produced the best automobiles of the era. Some say there wasn't a bad looking car made that year. The competition was tough and the big corporations could

*Kimes and Clark, Standard Catalog, 2nd ed., 440. Dodge Brothers/Dodge 1914. From the beginning, Budd Company made bodies for the Dodge Brothers cars called the all-steel body. There was some wood for tack strips and top bows. In 1928, Budd had dies and presses big enough to stamp out the complete side of a car body in one piece.

This is a beautifully restored 1933 V-12 Franklin, known as the "Banker's Car" because the bank had taken over the company by then.

loose money on their top-of-the-line cars. Companies like Peerless,* Pierce,† Packard and Franklin didn't have a line of models ranging from the low price to the top to aid their bottom line.

The manufacturers tried to survive in different ways. Peerless shut down automobile production and went into the beer business. The Pierce Company tried to make the best automobiles ever, but the Silver Arrow was their final effort. Packard, with more resources than the others, went the route of making less expensive models.

*Kimes and Clark, Standard Catalog, 2nd ed., 418. Peerless made cars in Cleveland, Ohio, from 1900 to 1931.
†Kimes and Clark, Standard Catalog, 2nd ed., 257. Pierce Company made cars in Buffalo, New York, from 1901 to 1938. In 1933 they made the futuristic model called the Silver Arrow. They only made five of these models. Their other models continued until 1938.

Franklin, by this time, was taken over by the bank. Edwin McEwan was put in charge. Franklin had already designed and built a V12 engine and designed a car to put it in. McEwan threw out the car design and erected a big heavy model that weighed a ton more than the one already designed. This took away any performance advantage the V12 would have had over the existing six-cylinder models.

With the limited resources available and the poor performance and sales of the V12 model, McEwan went to "Plan B." He bought bodies from R.E.O. and put Franklin engines in them. This plan didn't do very well either, as they had basically a R.E.O. car with a higher price tag.

One can only speculate that the company could have survived if they had left H.H. Franklin in charge. It is doubtful the company could have lasted anyway, but with McEwan, in trying to go upscale and then downscale with the R.E.O.–based Olympic with so few resources available, it may really have been a waste of money.

I try to envision what I would have done if given the chance of being in the right place at the right time. Of course, hindsight is always more accurate, but if Peerless made beer and Elcar* made mobile homes, why couldn't Franklin have made lightweight industrial engines? They already had a good engine and all they would have had to do is to scale it down to one, two or four cylinders, depending on the need.

The company ended in 1934 after thirty-two years in the automobile manufacturing business. This is a brief story of the Franklin, but sufficient to share all or in part when people ask you about the car. Whatever make of car you own, real car aficionados like to know something about the company that made it. This is particularly true of lesser-known makes.

William S. Locke, Elcar and Pratt Automobiles: The Complete History (McFarland, 2000), 179. Elcar made automobiles in Elkhart, Indiana, from 1916 to 1931. After the automobile company closed its doors, a trailer company with the same name started making trailers in Elkhart, with some of the same people involved. Locke states that there wasn't a direct connection between the two companies.

The car on the left is an Olympic model with a R.E.O. body and Franklin front end.

The next point about the history is dealing with the particular year and model. As an example, shortly after I bought my 1928 Dodge Brothers back in 1972, I saw an ad for 1928 Dodge headlights for sale. The lights on the car had been changed with some after-market seal beam units. This was a common practice when these old cars were being used as daily transportation. I bought the headlights, only to learn a long time later that they weren't the right ones. They were headlights for a 1928 Dodge, but for a "Standard 6" and my car was a "Victory 6." This is obvious to me now, but thirty years ago I didn't know that I should learn about all of the models and what parts interchanged and what didn't. Car companies, then as now, will use the same parts year after year, even if the body style is a lot different. The chassis and running gear may be the same.

With the 1930 Franklin, there were two basic models. There was the 145 and the 147. Some of the body details are different, but the main difference is the wheelbase, which is 125" and 132", respectively. With this knowledge, you can see any part pertaining to the longer wheelbase won't fit the shorter wheelbase, but most everything else will. The 1929 Franklin looked a lot like the 1930. Here again, some research will help you find what parts are interchangeable and what parts are not.

This is a great help when looking for parts. I didn't have to limit myself to looking for a 1930 part but for a part that would fit the era in which it was used. Even the most particular restorer doesn't care if the part came from a car a year or two older, or newer, as long as it is the same.

In 1930, Franklin came out with their new engine. Engine parts from 1929 and earlier, wouldn't be interchangeable with the 1930 engine. (Franklin, however, did use the same basic six-cylinder engine until they closed in 1934.) So, if you are looking for engine parts or a complete engine, any made after 1930 will be the kind you want. There were some minor changes made during that time and, of course, the engine numbers won't be in the range that yours should be.

Another practice of the early automobile companies was to use up their old stock before switching to new stock for their new models. My Franklin was body number thirty-nine, which would put it early in the 1930-model year. For 1930, the cars had different wheels: the same bolt pattern and size as before, but with a larger hub and shorter spokes. Several club members at a Trek I went on pointed out that I had 1929 wheels on my car. They were right as far as the model goes, but, because it was turned out early in the model year, my car could have came with 1929-style wheels. So, it would still be correct.

Another change for the 1930 model was the fender lights. I noticed that about half of the 1930 cars at the trek I attended had 1929-style fender lights and the rest had what was considered the 1930-style lights. No one seemed to question the difference in the fender lights, but they sure did the wheels. Could it be the Franklin company had more left-over fender lights than wheels?

In summation, as far as restoring your car goes, be sure what model year you have. Learn what you can of that model year and the years before and after. What changes were made and what stayed the same? This will give you a bigger parts pool.

The history of your cars ownership isn't necessary for restoration, but it adds to the value if a famous person owned it. Those cars certified as Full Classic by the CCCA (Classic Car Club of America) often have documentation saying where the car was originally sold, who bought it and who the subsequent owners were up to the current owner. This adds value as well as interest. The life history of the car can tell you not only who owned it, but also where it was kept and if any modifications or restoration work has been done to it. In some instances, like a Model J Duesenburg, the factory recalled the early models and replaced the aluminum connecting rods with steel ones. This detail would be covered in the car's documentation.

Of course, most of us don't have the big Full Classic or rare cars with a documented history. In this case, even if you knew who had owned the car, it wouldn't add value, but may add interest. I see ads sometimes where they say that they are the second or third owner. I don't care, unless they are the original owner with the original title. An old title has value in itself and even more so if you have the car to go with it.

I like to speculate about the history of a particular car. My 1928 Dodge was a four-door sedan. One could have concluded that when it was new, it was someone's family car. When I bought the car, I learned a preacher in Oregon had used it up to 1965, but when I was restoring it, I found some bullet holes in it. With some imagination, one could come up with several possible stories. Probably the truth would be even better if it was known.

The man that I bought the Franklin from got it from a farm in California. He said that it hadn't been drivable in twelve years. It looked like it had sat out in the weather longer than that. It did have 1954 license plates on it. The car must have had a hard life as it had a heavy-duty hitch on the back, the type that you would use to pull a farm wagon with. In restoring it, I noticed that the right rear axle tube had been welded with a piece of pipe inserted inside for reinforcement. In fact, the left side of the axle tube was reinforced the same way. One of the wheels was missing, which makes me think that at sometime it had hit something hard enough to break the axle and ruin the wheel.

This is only speculation, of course, but a plausible explanation. If the car could talk I bet it would have some interesting stories.

Where do I start when I am ready to do the research? Car clubs, as mentioned before, are a good place to start. There are books available for most makes of automobiles. If there is not one currently in print for your make of car, check antique or vintage automobile literature on the Internet. Other sources of literature are advertised in the same publications as automobiles. Museums are a good source of information, which brings us to the next chapter.

CHAPTER 3

Museums

You may ask, what does a museum have to do with restoring a car? I wanted to include this chapter in the book because I feel that there are several reasons.

First, most of the larger museums have a library with invaluable information. You can't just walk in and check out a book, though, like you would in a public library. But for a fee the staff will do some research for you. Most museums aren't a profitable business anyway, but the research work that they do helps keep the lights turned on.

I donated to the Harrah's Foundation Museum in Reno, back when Harrah's Automobile Collection was being sold. Some of the cars were donated to the Foundation, who was planning to erect a building to house the cars. They were accepting donations for this project and I remember that if you donated a certain amount, it entitled you to so many hours of research time. I never took advantage of the offer, but had I needed to glean some information then, the museum's library was available for me.

Secondly, if you are an old car buff like myself, a museum trip is the best vacation you can take. When I was young and single, back in the early 1960s and living only about an eight-hour drive from Reno, I would go there and tour the museum as often as time and money would allow. This was an exciting place to go back then. (In time the casinos and the shows gave way to the car museum.) I would spend the whole weekend at the museum. I watched its collection grow from about fifty to fifteen hundred cars on the floor. I was told that they also had another fifteen hundred in storage just waiting to be restored.

In time, they opened up the shops for visitors so that you could watch the restoration process. I learned a lot about restoring and was so interested that I even inquired about a job. I believed that I had the skills, but lacked the experience and knowledge. In the long run, I didn't feel that I could give up my day job to do this; this is one of the regrets that I have in life. The pay wasn't that good, but the experience would have been priceless.

I was married the last time that I went through the museum and my poor wife's eyes glazed over after spending all day looking at the old cars. She said that after awhile they all looked the same to her. What she didn't know was at least one or more old cars would be a part of our family for the next thirty-five years and that she would make at least two cross-country trips, plus assorted short jaunts, with one.

It was a sad day when I went to the first of several auctions that were held to sell off most of the Harrah's Automobile Collection. The one good thing about the auction was that people got a chance to really look the cars over. In the museum, they were all cleaned and roped off. At the auction, they were out so that it was possible to open the hoods, crawl under them and other stuff. After all a person is not going to buy a car if they can't look it over. The staff must have thought I was going to buy them all as I looked over and under so many of them in order to glean as much knowledge as I could.

The most expensive automobiles had guards watching over them. I didn't appear to have the resources to be buying one of them, so they were hesitant to let me look through them. As the old saying goes, if you can't dazzle them with brilliance, baffle them with B.S. I soon had the guards opening the hoods and doors for me. This was my first chance to really look at the cars like a Marmon sixteen cylinder or a model S.J. Duesenberg.

One of the highlights of the museum was the Franklin collection. Harrah's had at least one Franklin car for each year of production from 1903 to 1934. There were a total of sixty-five Franklins in all.

What I didn't know at the time, or until I began to take more interest in the Franklins, was that some of these cars were restored by Thomas H. Hubbard of Tucson, Arizona. He was considered the foremost authority on Franklins and he owned several of them himself. He was the principal person behind the founding of the H.H. Franklin Club. Besides being an expert restorer, he created the V12 Franklin from the original blueprints that the factory had. This was the car Franklin was going to build before the bank took over the company.

Mr. Hubbard passed away in 1993, leaving his home and his Franklin collection to the club. The H.H. Franklin Foundation was created to operate the museum. As other donated cars materialized, it outgrew the Hubbard home and property. The Foundation has been collecting donations for a new museum and I learned just recently that the Foundation purchased some property near Cazenovia, New York, for the purpose of building the museum there. When this happens, the Franklin Museum will move from Tucson, Arizona.

All of the cars of the great Harrah's Automobile Collection are still around somewhere. Some of them made it to other museums. The Harrah's Foundation in Reno has over three hundred of them. Most, I am sure, ended up with private owners and maybe some day they will end up in a museum again. I say this, not because I don't think people should own them, but my generation is passing on and the younger generation's interest is in cars that are of a newer era but still old to them. Therefore, older people like some Franklin owners are donating their cars to the museum.

Museums are a great source of information for the restorer, as well as entertaining. Some, like the Henry Ford museum in Dearborn, Michigan, have all manner of artifacts dealing with power and transportation.

Thirdly, museums are a source for buying an antique automobile. Almost all car publications will have ads with cars for sale by museums. Some even have a website for this purpose.

Make sure that you don't limit yourself to the ads. Visit a

museum and ask to talk to the curator, or whomever is in charge. Museums buy complete collections and sometimes get cars that they don't really want just to get the ones that they do want. They also get donations of cars that they don't want to display and so sell them to help raise money. Most museums want to display automobiles that are completely restored, unless leaving it as is makes sense for historical reasons. Unless it is a high-priced automobile, the cost of having it restored is more than the value of the car itself. This is the reason that museums sell some of their unrestored cars. For the person wanting to restore a car for the fun and enjoyment of it, the cost-to-value ratio is secondary. (Another reason museums sell their automobiles is that they are changing from automobiles to some other type of exhibit.)

When a museum or private collector holds an auction there is a chance to pick up a good buy. If the auction is well advertised and a buying crowd shows up, people get caught up in the enthusiasm and overbid a cars' value. This is a reason in itself to study the crowd, the auctioneer and the prices being paid.

I would recommend doing your research on the value of the car that you are interested in before going and don't get caught up in the excitement of the auction crowd. Everyone wants top dollar for what they are selling, but don't know the real value of what they have. If they set the reserve too high, no one bids on their car. If you approach that disappointed seller in a polite manner, he may sell you the car outright after the auction. After all, he has just learned it is not worth as much as he thought it was. You don't have to get a real steal, but if your resources are limited, the more you spend for the car, the less you have to restore it. In my opinion, auctions are fun and exciting, but I would rather buy a car directly from the owner.

In conclusion, check out the museums for fun and education. Ask if they have, or are going to have, any cars for sale. Ask if you can get on their mailing list in case something comes up in the future. Read the ads in car magazines and compare prices of similar models. Take your time in actually making your purchase. That way you can avoid buyer's remorse.

CHAPTER 4

Body Wood Restoration

I was going to give this car a ground-up restoration. That means a complete job from the ground up, but being the contrary person that I am, I decided to work from the top down. The body, and particularly the body wood, looked like the biggest single part of the restoration project. Either way, whether I did the chassis first or the body, the next step was to separate the both of them.

In the case of the Franklin, where the perimeter wood was missing and the body was extremely flexible, I had to determine some measurements first. By pulling the body together with straps and then wedging the doors until they lined up and then jacking up the right front corner of the car, I got the body fairly straight. I measured from hard points like the door, post irons along each side at the top of the car, then measured diagonally to make sure that it was not in a twist, or out of square. By drawing a chalk line from the windshield post to the rear doorpost on each side, I could determine how much of a curve there was supposed to be in the upper sill. I then measured across the top to establish the correct width, this being determined because I had the doors all fitting properly. I drew a picture looking down on the top of the car and wrote down all the measurements that I could, being careful to note exactly where the measurement was taken. I am not too concerned about the vertical measurements at this time because all the doorposts are there and I will measure from them as needed.

I removed the hood, grill, doors, seats, fenders and running boards in that order. Then, I disconnected all the connections

31

between the body and chassis and engine controls like the throttle, choke, clutch, steering column, brakes, wiring, and instruments. Now I was able to roll the car around and spot it to where I wanted to work on the body. I removed the body-to-chassis bolts and lifted the body off with a couple of come-alongs. Since the body was about as rigid as a wet rag, I had to lift it very carefully. I rolled the chassis out from under the body and let the body down on some sawhorses.

One could restore the chassis and engine first, then the body, but I decided to do the body first. My reasoning is that I like the chassis and engine work, so I saved the best for last. It is a psychological thing. I continued to disassemble the body, removing the dash panel, windshield frame and center door posts.

I inspected all of the wood in the body and found that most of it needed replacing except for the area around the rear window and the left rear corner of the car. As with most wood-framed bodies, the wood frame is made first and then the metal skin is placed over it. I didn't want to remove all of the metal skin, as I would lose the dimensions that I would need; therefore, it was necessary to work from the inside. This created another problem as a lot of the bracing iron is screwed to the wood under the body skin. By removing the lower body sill and front door post together I then could remove the iron later. At the rear of the sill behind the wheel well I had to pry the iron out and saw the screws off. With the front door post out, this let me drop the whole sill under the body.

The next difficulty I had to overcome was finding hardwood lumber in the dimensions that I needed. The body wood, as in most cars of this era, is ash. Ash, like other hardwood, comes in measurements 4, 5, 6, 8 quarters and up. Each number refers to the number of ¼-inch measurements of the wood's thickness before planning. For example, ¼ equals a 1-inch thick board. One must special order

Opposite top: **Here car body is strapped together and lined up in order to get some measurements to work with later.** *Bottom:* **As this photo shows, I don't have much top wood to use for patterns.**

This was for a 1930 Marmon Coupe. It is the first car that I did extensive body wood replacement. The old wood was good enough for patterns.

ash thicker than ¾-inch — 2 inches — which costs a lot of money and takes a long time to get.

The sills on the body were 2⅛-inches thick. I sorted through the ash at the lumberyard and found some rough-sawn 2⅛-inch boards, but the best I could do was to plane it down to 2-inches. Now, it is easier to find gold in Arizona than a straight board. The boards I had were all flat grained and crooked. I sawed them into 2 ¼-inch strips, 2-inches thick; I then turned them on edge and glued them back together. Then I went ahead and planed it down to 2⅛-inches, which gave me a straight, vertical-grained, laminated board in which to cut the sills. A glued-up board is stronger and more stable that a solid piece of the same size.

If you need to glue up some lumber for one side of the car, you may as well make the same blank for the other side at the same time

This shows the new laminated body sills. From top to bottom: the left sill blank, the right sill blank and then the original right sill.

if both need replacing. This will save some time, plus ensure that you have enough lumber to finish the job. I also recommend blanking out the longest pieces first. If the lumber that you have on hand is too thin or narrow, you can glue it up, but if it is too short, there is not much that you can do but to get more lumber. This, of course, is common sense, but it does take some planning to get the maximum utilization out of your lumber.

Check the old pieces (in this case the sill) and determine which side is supposed to be straight and flat, then look to see which sides or edges are 90 degrees to the flat straight side. This sill is just a flat plank (top and bottom, parallel). The inside edge is 90 degrees to the top and bottom with a slight curve to the right, then to the left. Lay the old piece on your new lumber and mark the inside line. Be sure that you have enough width to work with. If some of the old wood is rotted away, just mark what you have and fill in with a straight edge or follow the obvious curve on a curved piece. On a curved piece, if in doubt, leave it a little full, and then work it down later when you test for fit. The outer edge is 78 degrees from the top below the doors and rotates to 86 degrees at the firewall. The notch for the wheel well is 90 degrees, except at the forward edge. Mark the wheel well out. Be sure to use the maximum length for your lateral cut at the forward edge. Take your combination square, set it for just under 2⅛-inches and use a ⅜-by-⅜-inch block about 1 inch long to fill in the rabbet on the old sill. Slide the square and block along, keeping it perpendicular to the curve with your pencil at the inside corner of the blade. You can just freehand in the doorpost. Set your band saw at 90 degrees and make all of the cuts on the inside of the sill and at the wheel well. This will reduce the weight while you are still working flat. Now set the saw at a 78-degree angle. Start cutting at the front (be sure that your angle is right), stay about ⅜-inch outside of the line to allow for the 86 degree angle, then move to the line as you approach the area of the front door post. Dress up the edge and make the rotational in the cowl section with a plane and belt sander and trim the lateral cut at the wheel well; the sill should fit in place.

On the Franklin, though, this technique didn't work. I had to chisel some wood away to clear the front body mount, and mark and cut the overall length at the rear. I installed a couple of screws at each end to hold the sill in place temporarily, and located and marked the doorpost notches and irons. Removing the sill again, I used the router and cut the rabbet at the top outer edge and the relief for the iron bracing. The next step was to paint the sill with boiled linseed oil, thinned with turpentine. (Actually, any weather seal for wood will work.)

I have described the process of laying out and cutting the body sill in some detail as an illustration of what is involved. You would then go through the same steps with the front doorposts, remembering to measure and work from the flat side if you have one; in this and most cases, you will. Match the rabbets and reliefs as close to the old wood as possible. After you have completed a new piece, save the old one until you have the new one installed. This will help in locating it exactly within the body. Sometimes all you have to go on is a nail hole in relation to a relief, as measured from the old piece.

Clean up the iron bracing by removing the loose rust with a scraper and wire brush. Don't worry about removing all of the rust and leave the surface rough. Then paint all of the remaining iron bracing that you have left with a rust inhibitor paint, which usually works best on rusty metal.

I cut a couple of patch panels for the cowl area out of 14-gauge, lightly rusted metal. With some of the paint I glued them in place on the inside of the body while I had the wood out of the way. I used C-clamps to hold them in place for several days. Once the

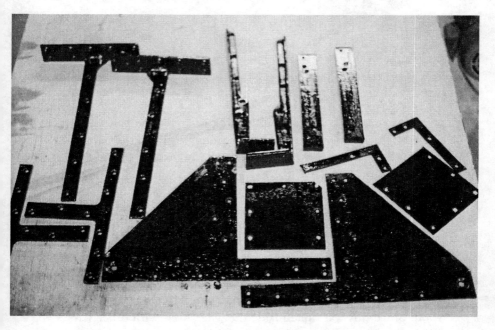

This is all the iron bracing that will be attached to the sills and doorposts after I had removed the rust and painted it with anti-rust paint.

This is the left body sill with the front door post attached and ready to install back into the car body.

paint has cured it is almost impossible to remove the panels unless you heat the metal with a torch hot enough to burn the paint.

After the paint had dried on the iron bracing, I fastened the front doorpost to the sill and slid it back into the body, doing this on both sides of the car. At the rear fender well where I sawed the screws off, I couldn't put the screws back in under the skin. I didn't want to remove the brace as it is riveted to the body, so I located the holes on the outside of the skin and inside the wheel well and drilled a ⅛-inch hole through the skin. I then ground a large center and punched the same angle as the screw heads and counter sunk the holes, and then put the screws through the skin and bracing into the wood. Since this was done inside the wheel well with other screws that just hold the skin to the wood, I felt a few more screw heads showing wouldn't make much difference.

I then removed the rear doorpost on the right side and the other rotten wood attached to it. I had to be careful to keep each piece intact as much as possible. Using each piece for a pattern, I cut new ones. I checked for fit as I went and used the opposite side of the car to help with the location of each piece. After all of the pieces I removed were made, I installed them in the car and checked that everything lined up and fit correctly. I screwed the joints together from the inside, making sure that the screws weren't too long to punch the skin. Once everything fit the skin went back in place. I disassembled the pieces and glued the joints and reassembled them, using the same screws.

After I had the wood replaced on the right side, I went to the left side and did the same thing. I only tacked the skin in place enough to keep the location accurate.

Next, I temporarily installed the doors on the new posts, checking the alignment. With the hinge side of the doors correct and the vertical alignment adjusted, I then installed the center doorpost, making sure that it centered between the front and rear doors and measured where the top of the post would have to be, both fore and aft and across from each other. I checked these measurements with my original measurements before disassembly and found them virtually the same.

I removed the doors and sat the car body on the shop floor. I leveled the body laterally at the front and back to make sure that it wasn't in a twist, and measured diagonally to check to make sure that it wasn't racked. With the body square, flat and low enough, I was ready for the top perimeter wood.

The first piece I made was the windshield header that is located, of course, between the front doorposts. These posts are steel from the cowl up and the header holds them the correct distance apart.

The rest of the top wood was ninety percent missing so I had to guess as best as I could, but I had a lot to go on. The metal skin for the door headers showed the inside and outside contour. The door header is straight along the bottom with a curve at the center post. The rear body skin is still in place, so I just have to fit the

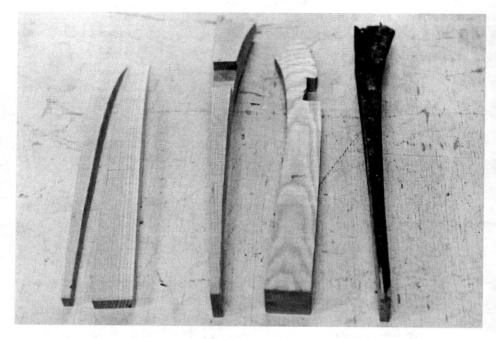

On compound curved pieces, cut one side and then tape the scrap back in place. Turn your block 90 degrees and make the second cut. Left to right: a double-cut scrap, then the new part that I am making, then the new cut scrap, and finally the original piece.

wood under the body skin and along the doorpost. The roundness along each side will match up with the rear body and the windshield header with an even transition in between. I also know that the inside of the door headers are square with the bottom and even with the inside of the door post, due to the shape of the bracing iron.

There was a short piece of wood on the left side that went from under the body skin to a joint above the rear door. Using this for a pattern, I made a new one as close to the original as I could and, with some trial and error, I eventually got it to fit. I then made the same piece for the right side by using the contour of the left with the angles the opposite way.

This is the roughed-in left side door header. Note the shim under the corner brace at the windshield header.

With these pieces mortised in place to the rear doorpost, I continued working on the header to the windshield. By checking the lateral measurements with my original ones, I determined how much dogleg to put in the header. I made a pattern out of a piece of ¼-inch scrap plywood — by turning it over I could use it on both sides of the car. The header was cut from ⅜-inch ash with the sides left square. I cut a notch out for the lap joint at the rear piece and cut a mortise for the center doorpost. After installing these headers, I glued on a filler strip to give me enough thickness to match the rear piece. Then, using my power planer, I contoured the header from the rear, working down the taper to the front. After roughing it in, I used the belt sander to smooth up the radius and contour of the top and outside surfaces. When I had the left side satisfactory, I made three templates of the cross section at the center post and the center of each door. Using the templates, I worked the right-side header down as close as possible to the left side.

I now had the top perimeter wood in place. I next installed all of the bracing irons at the doorpost and was ready for the top bows. From the short piece of original top wood, I had determined the first two bows from the rear were about 7 inches apart and the next was 9 inches. I measured from that point to the windshield header and it came out close to 9 inches on center for the rest of the bows. I also noticed a rabbet ⅝-inch wide and 1/16-inch deep on the short piece of the original wood. I concluded that it was for the chicken wire, so the next step was to cut the rabbet around the inside of the perimeter. I located and cut the notches for the bows with the router.

I made the bows out of ⁵/₄-inch ash and cut them all 54 inches long with a 1-inch rise, as the bows got shorter toward the front. I kept the center line aligned and trimmed each end to fit, which brought the rise down to ⅝-inch at the windshield header. In doing this, I maintained a uniform crown on the car top. The bows were let in to match the bottom of the chicken wire rabbet. Before fastening the bows in place, I drilled holes for the dome light wires and made a mounting block for the dome light. Now that all the body wood was repaired or replaced, I gave it a coat of linseed oil.

I nailed the body skin and doorframe metal back in place. After removing the glass from the doors (to make them lighter), I temporarily hung the doors to locate the hinge screw holes and to determine how much to shim the hinges if it was necessary. With the doors aligned, I could install the door striker plates and latches. I removed the doors and marked at the hinge reliefs how much shim, if any, I might need. (I did need 1/32 or 1/16 of an inch.)

I mentioned before that I removed the door glass, so with the doors disassembled, I checked the condition of the wood and found it to be in good shape, except for some minor repair. At this time I checked the window regulators and door latches and also saved some of the old window channels so that I could order new channels with the same cross-section measurements.

This is with the body wood replaced. I haven't painted the top wood with linseed oil yet. I used some of the old filler strips on the doorposts.

I could now sandblast the body and do any bodywork and also paint it. I decided to start on the chassis, as I didn't want the finished body getting dinged up while I was working on the chassis. Also, all the parts that were to be painted the same color, I wanted to paint when possible, at the same time when possible.

With this thought in mind, I made a dolly out of some 2 × 4s and some heavy-duty casters and put the body on it and rolled it out of the way.

CHAPTER 5

Rebuilding the Engine

I rolled the chassis back into my shop and removed the engine, transmission and drive shaft. I then moved the chassis back outside so that it would be out of the way. After separating the engine and transmission, the next step was to disassemble the engine.

There are plenty of books out on how to overhaul an engine, down to the make and model. What concerns the old car restorers is how to rebuild the engine and keep it as original as possible but also dependable, though not necessarily for 100,000 miles at today's speeds. Parts for antique engines are a lot more expensive than for a modern engine and your antique car probably won't be driven as your main transportation. I am speaking here, of course, of a 1930s vintage car. If you restore a 1960s or 1970s car, it will be considered a modern car for all practical purposes.

What I am attempting here is not so much to explain how to overhaul an engine, but to help the restorer decide if machine work is needed when a part needs to be replaced, or if he can make do with what he has.

Before the engine is disassembled, make sure the parts are marked so that they can be assembled back in the respective positions. It is really important, as an example, to get not only the main bearing caps back in their respective order, but to have them turned the right way. I generally stamp the main bearing caps, connecting rods and caps with a number stamp on the cam side so that I won't inadvertently get them turned around.

With the parts correctly marked, completely disassemble the

This pile of parts is the Franklin engine. Note that I have kept the pistons, cylinders and cylinder head together.

engine, including the cam bearing and soft plugs in the block. You need to have all of the parts off of the block that are not iron, so that the block can be hot-tanked at most any engine rebuilding shop. This is important, in order to get all of the crud out of the water jacket and oil passages. (The Franklin, of course, didn't have a water jacket or an internal oil rail, so I didn't take this step.) While you have your engine block and cylinder head at the engine shop, have them replace the exhaust valve seats with modern hard seats.

Most of these old engines didn't have hard seats and they have been ground too many times and are usually heat damaged (checked). I have found that you are ahead of the game just to have the block or head counter bored and hard seat installed. This should cost about $80.00 or so for a six-cylinder engine.

The Franklin has bronze seats in the aluminum heads so I

didn't need to do this, but my 1928 Dodge had to have 390 Ford hard seats installed.

Check the valve guides; most of the late 1920s and early 1930s have removable valve guides. With a model A Ford you have to remove the guides in order to remove the valves, as they have a

This is a Dodge-6 cylinder block with 390 cubic inch Ford hard seats installed for the exhaust valves.

mushroom stem. If your guides are worn and are not a replaceable part, have the engine machine shop bore out the guides and re-sleeve them. This isn't a very expensive operation. You may be able to purchase new valves with oversized stems. If so, you will need to ream the guides to fit.

How much is too much valve stem clearance? These questions are always a judgment call, but for those slow-turning engines you can get by with .005-inch to .006-inch slop in the guide. I know other books will say .001-inch or .002-inch, but we are trying to keep the cost down and still have a reasonable life expectancy and dependability from the engine. A flat head engine can have more wear than an overhead valve engine for two reasons: (1) The oil drains away from the valve stem instead of down it, and (2) The rocker arm motion on the overhead valve tends to put a side thrust on the valve stem so the wear tends to egg-shape the guide, which then makes the valve rock in the seat.

Grinding the valves needs to be considered at this time. If you don't have a valve grinder, have the shop do this for you also. I prefer to do my own, because most shops think in terms of fast production and don't want to take the time to fool around like I do. I like to grind the seats in what is called a three-angle valve job; say 30 degrees — 45 degrees — 60 degrees. This way, the area where the valve seats can be uniform in width, at about .050-inch to .070-inch. That is narrow enough to cut the carbon and wide enough to dissipate the heat. Then grind the valve (if the seat is 45 degrees) at 44 degrees. This will ensure the outer edge is in contact with the seat. Lap the valve in. This will show exactly where the valve and seat contact, which should be .030-inch to .040-inch from the edge

From left to right: a 390 cubic inch Ford exhaust valve, the Ford valve with the Dodge keeper groove cut into it and the original Dodge exhaust valve.

of the valve. If the valve has to be ground to a sharp edge to clean it up, it should be replaced. A valve that is too thin on the edge will heat check. I am speaking of exhaust valves, but even the intake valves that are too thin will cup out and you won't be able to maintain your valve lash adjustment.

If you need to replace any of the valves, it is quite a bit more expensive to have them custom made. There are several suppliers that will have N.O.S. (New Old Stock) valves or they can make them to fit your engine. But check first to see if you can find modern valves. I just rebuilt someone else's 1928 Dodge six-cylinder engine this way. From experience working on my own 1928 Dodge six, I learned to install 390 cubic-inch Ford hard seats.

I knew the valves would fit the seat, but would the stem diameter and length fit? I bought one valve for about five dollars to check the fit. I was lucky in that the diameter was just right and the length just a little too long. There was enough adjustment in the tappet to compensate for the added length. I checked the valve in my lathe and modified the stem to take the 1928 Dodge keepers and valve-spring retainers. It worked so well that I bought five more valves at about one-fourth the cost of N.O.S., or custom valves.

I like to check through the parts books at automobile machine shops. Suppliers give these books to the shops and sometimes I have had the shops give me their old copies. If you have this opportunity to look through these books, in this case for valves, look for a valve with the right stem diameter. The stem should be long enough or too long. The head diameter can be just right or a little too big. By grinding the head down and cutting the stem off and making new keeper grooves, you can make a valve fit your old engine.

This may sound like a lot of work, but it does save money, plus you get a better quality valve than the original. Just be sure that you use exhaust valves to replace old exhaust valves or intake valves. But do not use intake valves to replace old exhaust valves.

Another thing to check while doing the valve work is the tappets. This is often overlooked when rebuilding an engine. The problem is that the tappets wear down where they contact the valve stem, giving them a concave surface. This in itself doesn't diminish the engine's performance, except that you can't check the valve-to-tappet clearance, or valve lash. The feeler gauge will bridge over the hollowed-out portions of the tappet and you will have more clearance than indicated by the feeler gauge. The solution, of course, is to grind the tappet head flat. This can be done with almost all valve-grinding machines. The same problems exist to a lesser degree with overhead valve engines. In this case, grind the pad at the end of the rocker arm where it contacts the valve stem.

The cylinders need to be evaluated while the block is at the machine shop. If you bore the cylinders, then you will need new pistons. Fit the new piston pins to the connecting rods. (Pretty soon you will be talking real money. Any fool can put an engine together if he has got enough money, but this is a hobby and not a government operation.)

Again, how much cylinder wear is too much?

If you don't have a set of inside micrometers, you can get a good indication of cylinder wear and taper using a piston ring. Take the rings off of a piston and place one of the compression rings in the bore using the piston to keep the ring square in the bore; push it down to the top of the ring travel area. Measure the ring and gap with feeler gauges — let us say that it is .090-inch — then push the ring down in the cylinder below the ring travel area and measure the end gap — and it's .030-inch. Subtract the two measurements — in this case .060 — then divide by pi or 3. This will give you .020-inch. If your cylinders are worn this much, you will have to bore the cylinders oversize and get new pistons and rings. The rings expanding and contracting as they move up and down the taper will cause them to fatigue and break, plus they won't seal very well.

A cylinder that is in real poor condition can be bored and sleeved back to the original diameter if your pistons are good enough. This may be cheaper than buying oversized pistons.

The next best scenario is that you have less than .010-inch cylinder wear. Hone the cylinder, giving extra time to the lower part in order to straighten the cylinder as much as you can. When installing new rings, be sure to check the end gap, which should be about .020-inch at the top and bottom of the ring travel area. If the gap is too close, grind the end of the ring until you get the clearance you need. If there is too much end gap, go to oversized rings.

The piston will probably be too loose; you should have .003-inch to .005-inch clearance at the skirt at right angles to the piston pin. But if you don't, aluminum pistons can be knurled to expand the diameter. Some of the old engines with solid skirt pistons (not split skirt) can be flattened out of round with a leather strap and a mallet. Don't try this with cast iron pistons!

Over all your best hope is that the pistons and cylinders aren't worn very much. In this case, hone the cylinder just enough to break the glaze and then buy new rings. Be sure to check if the engine has oversized pistons. If so, be sure to get the oversized rings. To check the piston pin bushing wear, or wear in the piston boss, hold the piston and push and pull on the connecting rod. If you can feel any movement, the pin is too loose. The type with bushings in the rod can be replaced and honed to size. If the pin rotates in the piston, then you will have to get new pistons with the full floating type. You may need both.

There are several companies that make custom pistons for about any engine ever made, but they cost around $50.00 each. The two most important measurements of a piston are the bore size and the compression height. This height is the distance from the pin center to the top of the piston. If you were lucky enough to find a newer engine with the same piston measurements that were readily available, the piston would cost less than half as much.

Okay, what do you do? The cylinders are marginal, the pistons are questionable, and you are not sure about the piston pins. I would say, if in doubt, bore them out. Buy new pistons and fit the pins; just don't tell the wife how much it cost.

I have covered the upper part of the engine, but the more critical and expensive part can be the lower or bottom end. Of course, check the complete engine over before deciding on what to replace and what to salvage. For example, if the connecting rods needed piston pin bushings, you would check the rod bearings to determine if they need to be rebabbitted in order to decide on the rod bearing diameters. You will need to determine if the crankshaft needs ground undersizing.

You have to comprehend the entire situation in order to make an intelligent decision. If money is no object, just replace everything, but I believe a mechanic needs to figure out what the life

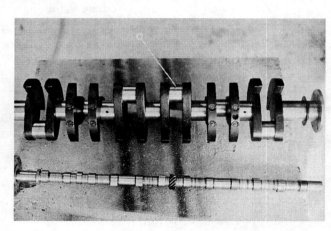

On top is a Franklin crankshaft with a brush in the oil passage. Below is the Franklin camshaft cleaned and polished.

expectancy of a part is. When I was rebuilding heavy equipment in the logging and heavy construction trade, the first question I would ask customers is how long they intended to keep the particular piece of equipment I was servicing. With this knowledge, I could make a better decision on how much life to build back into the engine, transmission, etc. The same approach will apply to your collector car. Only you can determine how much you are going to drive it and, of course, how much you want to spend.

The lower end of the engine consists of the crankshaft, camshaft and related parts. What if you have an overhead cam engine? Isn't that the upper half? Yes, but remember we are dealing with production car engines of an earlier era. A few engines of this period had D.O.H.C. (Dual Overhead Cam), like the Miller racing engines and the Model J Duesenberg, but most were flathead or side-valve engines and a few makes had push-rod valves-in-head engines.

Clean the crankshaft up and be sure to run a brush through the oil passages if it has any. If the engine hasn't been run in a long time, resist the temptation to start it up before you tear it down. The crankshaft may have rusted, and running it would do more damage to the bearings. With a crankshaft that is rusted extensively, the journals are rough and grooved or are hammered out of round due to a loose rod and will need to be repaired. In this case, you will have to have the main bearings and the connecting rods rebabbitted.

If you need to rebabbitt all of the rod bearings, it may be better to have them bored out and modern insert bearings installed. In V6 and V8 engines, the bearings are usually too large in diameter and too narrow to substitute in an old engine. Look up bearing sizes on in-line six, four or small diesel, and other industrial engines.

In most connecting rods of this era, the babbitt-bearing material is poured directly into the rod, then machined to size with shims between the connecting rod and cap for later adjustment.

The main bearings were sometimes poured into the block, but by the 1930s it was more common to babbitt steel or bronze inserts.

In either case, the bearings were installed in the block with shims under the caps, then aligned and bored to the main bearing journals diameter plus the oil clearance.

I was lucky with this Franklin in that the crankshaft was in fairly good shape and there were shims left in the connecting rod bearings.

The bearing shells (or inserts) on a modern engine are a little longer in circumference than needed to fill the bore of the bearing. The reason is that when the bearing caps are torqued down, this forces the bearing shell tight in the bore with some crush area at the junction of the upper and lower halves. These old engines with the heavy bearing inserts, either bronze or steel-backed, will not crush under the normal torqued load; therefore, it is important to check their fit.

Clean the bearing bore area to make sure that no rust or foreign material can cause a high spot in the bore. Polish the crankshaft journals with emery cloth or stiff-backed paper abrasive. I used a 350 grit. Cut one piece a little narrower and shorter than the journal circumference. Use a light oil (WD 40) on the abrasive, wrap it around the journal, take a leather thong and make one or two wraps around the abrasive and pull the ends back and forth. Pull at different angles and rotate the crankshaft to about three different positions. After going over all of the surfaces lightly with the 350 grit, I repeated the process with the 500-grit abrasive. This gave me a well-polished bearing surface.

The engine had sat so long without being run that the bearing material had oxidized to form a real hard surface. I rubbed this off with the 350 grit and oil, and then polished the bearing with the 500 grit. If you have to do this, be sure and keep the bearing flat across and only take off what you need to clean it up.

After cleaning up any part with an abrasive, be sure to wash it thoroughly with hot soapy water. This will remove any abrasive out of the pores of the metal better than a solvent.

With the engine upside down, place all of the main bearing inserts in the block (or crankcase, as I did with the Franklin), being careful to put them back in their respective positions. Smear a little white grease in the bearings and carefully lay the crankshaft in place. Be sure to check the endplay of the crankshaft. If the front main is the thrust bearing part, this can be adjusted later, but if it is one of the intermediate bearings that takes the thrust, you may have to shim the face bearings at this time to a .004-inch to .006-inch endplay.

On these old Dodge six engines, the front main bearing takes the thrust. The bearing has a slot that fits over a dowel in the block. The dowel prevents the bearing from rotating in the bore, but it is held fore or aft only by the clamping force of the bearing cap. The idea appears to be that you can adjust the bearing fore or aft until the crankshaft is centered in the block. There is a faceplate on the end of the crankshaft that you adjust with shims to get the correct endplay.

I have rebuilt three of these Dodge engines and all of them had too much crankshaft endplay because the front main bearing moves ahead in the bore. The clamping force of the bearing cap isn't enough to hold the bearing in position.

This is the main bearing that was oxidized (below), so I polished them to clean them of the corrosion. These are white brass bearings; the babbit would probably be fatigued and cracked.

For this problem I devised a solution by centering the crankshaft in the block and then sliding the front main bearing aft until the flange on the bearing contacts the crankshaft. Then measure the distance between the inside of the bearing flange and the bearing web in the block. I found that it is usually fifty to sixty-thousandths of an inch. Cut enough shims to take up the space that fits over the bearing, but behind the flange. To install, first adjust your front main bearing as you normally would. After removing all of your main bearing caps, lift the crankshaft with the upper and lower front-bearing shells. Slide the ring-type shims you have made over the bearing shells and lower it back into place. Put the bearing cap back in place and then you slide the crank-

This is my solution to keep the Dodge front main bearing in place by adding shims behind the face flange.

shaft and bearing tight against the shims. This will give you a positive adjustment on centering your crankshaft and prevent the clutch from forcing the crankshaft forward in the engine.

While you may never work on a 1928 Dodge six engine, the procedure I've described to ensure the crankshaft stays in place should work with similar engine designs.

(Note: Before disassembly of any engine, check to make sure that the crankshaft is in the correct position in the first place. The connecting rods should be centered on the piston pins and there should be end clearance on all of the main bearings.)

Next, put an insert in the cap and seal a little grease on the bearing surface and put a strip of Plastigage just off center in the bearing. Slide the bearing and cap down over the studs (most all old engines used studs instead of cap screws) into the proper position. (You can start with any of the main bearings.) Tighten the nuts to about 10 foot-pounds, using a .002-inch feeler gauge. Check if there is any clearance between the block and cap. Be sure to check both sides.

With the Franklin, I had about .004-inch clearance with most of the bearing caps, so the next step is to remove the cap and see if the Plastigage squeezed down any. According to the Plastigage, it had around .003-inch clearance at the bearing. I removed the insert from the cap and filed the edges a little. I used a big flat single cut file, laid it flat on the workbench and slid the bearing insert on the file. Then I turned it around after a few strokes to make sure that it was being cut flat and even on each side.

I replaced the bearing and cap with the Plastigage and placed it back in position and repeated the procedure. This time the cap was less than .002-inch from the block, so I torqued the nuts down to about 85 foot-pound on those ½-inch studs. I then removed the cap again to check the Plastigage and found out that I had .0015-inch clearance, which is about right. With old engines you will want to have between .0015-inch and .002-inch oil clearance.

If the bearing cap does not contact the block on both sides, but your oil clearance is right, shim between the block and cap, but not the bearing insert. Torquing a cap down that doesn't make good contact will spring it out of round.

If the cap and the block make good contact, but you have too much oil clearance, shim between the insert and the cap. The shim should be about ¾ the length of the outside of the insert. On the main bearings always shim the cap side of the bearing, not the block side.

If the cap and block have good contact, but there is insufficient oil clearance, shim between the block and cap including the inserts.

Rotate the crankshaft after each bearing is adjusted; it should turn freely with just a little drag from the white grease, and have no tight spots. If the crankshaft rotates free, about half a turn, but tightens up half a turn, you have a journal out of round, or a bent crankshaft. If you can rotate it by hand without using any leverage, like a pry bar, it should be okay. But if it takes any significant effort, you need machine work or another crankshaft.

Now you need to cotter key or safety wire the studs and nuts. If the studs are locked into the block, cotter key the nuts; use safety wire if the studs are not locked in.

Remove all of the nuts from the main bearing caps, leaving the caps in place. Put a line across the end of the studs parallel to the cross-drilled hole. Install the two nuts on the bearing cap and torque to the low end of the range. (On this old iron I like to use 60-to-70 foot-pound on 7/16-inch studs and 80-to-90 foot pound on 1/2-inch

Here I marked the end of the studs with whiteout marker to help locate the cross drilled holes.

studs.) If a hole aligns with a slot in the castel nut, you are lucky, but if you're not, torque the nut down some more, but don't go over the high range. If you still don't get an alignment, try another nut. If you fool around long enough, eventually you will be able to cotter key or safety wire all of the nuts and studs. If the last couple of nuts won't line up, file the bottom of the nut.

Clean the camshaft and polish the lobes and journals with 400- or 500-grit emery cloth or heavy-paper abrasive. If you find the cam lobes are worn down there are several places that you can regrind your cam and, in some cars, improve the profile. In my experience with these old slow engines with light valve springs, the cams last pretty well. The cam bearings are another story, in that they tend to wear, especially the front bearing on a chain-driven cam. Most cam bearings in this era of engines are locked in, usually with a brass pin through the side of the block, so check first before removing them.

In the Franklin, the splash-oil-cam bearings are split, locked in with setscrews and have to be removed with the camshaft.

The most common cam oiling system for this era is for the oil to travel from the main bearing to the cam bearings. An engine with excessive wear in the cam bearings will not have good oil pressure, even if the crankshaft bearings are set up right.

The cam bearings are generally a ring of bronze or steel with babbitt-bearing material inside. Engines where the cam bearing can be removed only from the front of the engine are usually stepped, meaning the outside diameter is progressively smaller toward the rear of the engine. This is to facilitate installation, as there is a light press fit into the block and you don't want to drive the bearing through successive bores to install them.

If the cam bearings can be installed from inside the crankcase, they may all be the same diameter.

The cam bearings can be rebabbitted, but you will need to get an accurate bore diameter in the block for each bearing. This may be difficult to do, especially the intermediate bearings. I have found that they are usually an even fraction of an inch and the stepped type will go in even steps: like $\frac{1}{32}$ of an inch. Using a snap gauge and micrometer, you will probably get a slightly undersized measurement, but comparing your measurement with the decimal table, you will see that you are within a few thousandths of an inch to an even fraction, so a safe bet is that measurement is the correct one.

When installing the cam bearings, it is important to get the oil hole and the lock pinhole lined up. What worked well for me was to put the cam bearing in dry ice. This shrank it down to a loose fit. Then I slid it in place and then using a $\frac{1}{8}$-inch rod through the lock pinhole, I rotated the bearing until the rod slipped through the hole. Check to make sure that the oil hole is also open. You will have to work fast, or the cam bearing will warm up quick and get tight in the bore.

With the cam bearing in place, put a little white grease on them and slide the cam in. If everything is copasetic, it should rotate with a slight drag. If you can't turn it by hand, use a 1-inch by 2-inch wooden drift near the bearing on the camshaft and give it a good rap with a hammer. This helps align the bearing and cam and should free it up.

With the cam and crankshaft installed, the next logical step is the pistons and connecting rods. As mentioned before, check the piston ring end gap and adjust by grinding the ends of the rings to get a .005-inch gap per inch of cylinder bore. Install the rings on the pistons and, using a ring compressor, squeeze them down and push the piston in the bore.

With most engines, the big end of the connecting rod will fit through the bore of the cylinder. In this case, install the pistons from the top of the engine.

If the rods are too big to fit through the bore, then the piston will have to be installed from the bottom. If this is your situation, then install the piston and rods before you install the crankshaft, as there is usually limited room in the crankcase.

Check the rod journal diameters. On the Franklin they measured between 2.1235 inch and 2.124 inch. Then measure each connecting rod's big end bore with the cap tight and no shims along the longitudinal axles. The Franklin rods measured 2.115 inch to 2.117 inch. Subtract this measurement from the corresponding journal diameter and then add .001 inch for oil clearance. This will tell you how much shim that you will need.

If you are real confident in your measurements, your rod bearings should be okay. I like to over-shim and check with Plastigage and remove shims until I get the .001 to .0015 clearance that I need. By using this method, you don't take the risk of over-tightening the bearing and springing the cap.

It is best to have the same shims on each side of the rod, but a few thousandths of an inch difference won't compromise the bearings' life. For example: if you have .001-inch excessive clearance and the thinnest shim that you have is .002-inch, just take one shim of one side and this will take the clearance down to .001-inch.

With the crankshaft connecting rods and pistons and the camshaft all in place, now is a good time to set the valve timing.

Just align the timing works on the cam and crank. This will usually work, but are the marks in the right place and is the gear or sprocket positioned correctly on the cam? The Franklin has several

To check the wear of my timing chain, I wrapped it around the cam sprocket and held it tight. Then I pulled up on the opposite side. I shouldn't pull out more than ½ a tooth at the center (pull at the arrow).

bolt patterns that will change the timing considerably from one extreme to the other.

I have the *Motor Service and Specification Manual* (copyright MoToR, page 12) that covers from 1925 to 1932 models. This is how it explains the valve timing for the 1930 Franklin: "Remove the No. 1 spark plug and crank engine until No. 1 piston is coming up on the compression stroke and continue until it is at top dead center. Set the intake valve at .031-inch clearance and then insert a .005-inch feeler gauge under the valve stem. Turn the crankshaft almost one revolution, until the same tension is secured on the .005-inch feeler gauge that was on the .031-inch gauge. At this point, the ^ mark on the fan rim should be from ⅞-inch to 1¾-inch beyond the mark on the fan housing."

These directions may be good enough to check your engine timing, but of little use to set it in the first place. By following these directions, you have to install the timing cover, blower housing and blower. Then if your timing isn't right, you will have to remove all of these parts to reset the timing and then try again until you are lucky enough to get it right.

I will try to explain the method that I use. It will work for all engines, even if you don't have a timing mark.

On almost all four-cycle engines you will have two pistons top-dead center at the same time. (One exception is the early V6 Buick with the uneven firing.) Also, most timing is done with the number

Here I am checking the crankshaft to camshaft timing. (Note the dial indicator on number 1 cylinder and push rods in place on the number 6 cylinder.)

1 cylinder or its opposite. It is cylinders 1 and 4 for a four-cylinder car and cylinders 1 and 6 for a six-cylinder, etc. V-type engines have an opposite cylinder, but since the number is different for different makes, you will have to check your individual make. The opposite cylinder will be the one halfway through the firing order.

On the Franklin, I set the crank at the top-dead center for the No. 1 cylinder with a dial indicator. I installed the cylinder head on the No. 6 cylinder so that I could adjust the valves on that cylinder. Install valves only on your opposite cylinder or push rods in the case of overhead valve engines. (On overhead valve engines you will have to install the head.)

Set your normal valve clearance then rotate the cam so that it is between the exhaust closing and the intake opening. If you don't have any free travel at this point, readjust the valve lash .005-inch more until you get a degree or two of free travel. If you have too much free travel, tighten the lash adjustment until you can just feel a little rotation. The object is to get the cam centered between the lobes.

Advance the cam to take up the free travel. Remember, the chain drive cam turns the same direction as the crankshaft and the gear cam turns the opposite.

With the cam and crank set in position, install the chain or cam gear. The timing mark should be close to alignment or half a turn off on the cam gear or sprocket. Don't be concerned if you are half a turn off, as one rotation of the crankshaft will get you back in alignment. What we need to do here is make the fine adjustment to get the chain tight or the gears meshed.

Be careful not to turn the cam or crank, but move the cam gear or sprocket to fit the cam. With the Franklin, I just turned the sprocket until the chain was tight and used the bolt pattern that fit.

On some engines, you may have to elongate the bolt holes in the cam sprocket or gears. If it is keyed to the cam, you can make an offset key. The object here is to get the valve train in mesh without throwing the timing off.

Another way to set the valve timing is to use dial indicators. The advantage of this method is that all of the valves can be in place. With the crankshaft top-dead center on the No. 1 cylinder, adjust the valves to zero clearance on that cylinder, making sure you are off of the lobe. Set a dial indicator on each valve (flathead engine) or push rod (overhead valve engine) at zero. Turn the cam until you are between exhaust closing and intake opening. Rotate the cam back and forth until you get the same reading on each dial. If your dials are reading zero, advance the cam until the one on the intake just starts to move.

With the cam and crank set, proceed with the chain or gear installation.

I rechecked the Franklin after further assembly as prescribed by the motor manual, the timing and was right on: equal to about ½ a tooth advance on the cam compared to what it was when I first disassembled the engine.

Install the valves at this time if you have a flathead engine or the push rods on your overhead valve engine. Adjust the valve lash about .002-inch, more than recommended, as the valve tends to seat in and take up some of the clearance.

On bottom oil engines like the Franklin, install the oil rail and be sure that the restricted fittings are open. These usually will be found at the timing chain oiler and the return on the bypass filter.

Since I am restoring the Franklin for driving I modified the oil system to include a full-flow filter. The number one killer of these old engines is dirt, as they didn't have adequate crankcases or carburetor air filters during that era.

On engines with dipper oiling for the rod bearings, make sure that the dippers are installed correctly. In my youth, I took apart several old Chevrolet engines with the rod bearings out because someone put the dippers on backward.

Torque your head down using the stage method. Let us say that you have ⁷/₁₆-inch studs that you will torque to 70 foot-pounds. Go through your pattern at 50 foot-pounds and then repeat at 60 foot-pounds and then to the final 70 foot-pounds. For most of these old engines, it is recommended to re-torque after the engine is warmed up.

If you don't know the torque pattern, just start in the center and work toward the edge and each end, alternating across and end-to-end.

Engines with ³/₈-inch-head studs that are supposed to be torqued to 40-45 foot-pounds never seemed to hold the head gasket. I recommend going to grade-8 studs and torque the head at 50-55 foot-pounds.

Be sure to torque the flywheel bolts. If they are too loose, the torsion vibration will wallow out the holes and if they're too tight, they will put excessive strain on the bolts.

Well, the engine is just about back together except for the accessories and, of course, you will want to paint it.

The only gaskets that you need to buy are the head gasket and the manifold gaskets; the rest you can make. (See Chapter 12 on "Maintaining Your Car" for information on how to make your gaskets.) Use ⅛-inch cork for the rocker covers or tappet covers and ⅟₁₆-inch paper for the oil pan and thin paper for the water pumps and other water connections.

If you can't get a new head gasket but your old one isn't deteriorated, soak the old one in detergent and water. If you are in a hurry, boil it. This will swell up the asbestos core and then you can get a new squeeze on it.

Install the distributor with the cap off and crank the engine by hand until the No. 1 piston is near the top dead center at the end of the compression stroke. Removing the spark plug and feeling the air being forced out can determine this. While cranking the engine, note the direction of rotation of the rotor.

Now that the No. 1 piston is in firing position, replace the cap. If the rotor is not pointing in the direction of the No. 1 post, you have three options:

(1) If your distributor has a gear on the end of the shaft, pull the distributor and rotate the shaft and gear to index it to the correct position.

(2) If the distributor has a drive tang, loosen the clamp at the base and rotate the distributor housing until the rotor points to the No. 1 post on the cap.

(3) If you have a distributor that can't be rotated enough, shift the spark plug wires until you have the No. 1 wire on the post that the rotor is pointing toward.

After the No. 1 spark plug wire is in the cap, install the rest according to the firing order, being sure to use the correct rotation.

Old car rallies allow for later model distributors of the mechanical type. The material the old points were made of burned and pitted relatively fast. I modified a slant-six Dodge distributor for my 1928 Dodge. In the Franklin, I used modern points in the original distributor by filing the mounting holes to fit the distributor plate.

The Franklin doesn't have a water pump of course, since it is an air-cooled engine, but I have repaired quite a few so I will share my experience with the reader.

The water pump leaks on almost every old car that I see at car shows. The main reasons are poor design and poor materials.

The material in the pump shaft is vulnerable because it is made of mild steel and tends to rust. The rust makes the shaft rough, which then chews up the seal packing. When the packing wears out, water leaks out and air leaks in.

Some old timers have told me about their cars overheating because the water circulated too fast and so they cut some of the impeller blades off of the pump and figured that they had fixed the problem. They may have helped, but it didn't really. The problem is that the pump will draw air into the cooling system and the air forces the water out. By cutting the impeller blades off, the pump wasn't efficient enough to draw air in through the seal packing.

One fix to keep the water pump looking original is to make or buy a stainless steel pump shaft. This will stop the rust and the packing will last much longer. But the problem of trying to seal a shaft that has radial movement due to bushing wear will still exist, and the packing nut will have to be tightened periodically.

My method of repair in my Dodge was to change the design by using a ceramic seal from a domestic water pump. To replace the old packing nut I made a new nut that the ceramic part of the seal will fit into. Then the carbon and rubber part of the seal is placed on the shaft with a drive collar and the pump is reassembled.

The ceramic seal, since it is a face seal, isn't affected by radial movements of the shaft and will virtually never wear out. The total cost for my materials was less than $10.00. Of course, it doesn't look original if one looks that close, but it sure makes the car more drivable and it can always be changed back if the car is also for show.

Now you are ready to paint the oil pan and other covers. When

this is completed, install them along with the manifolds and other accessories. Now your engine should be ready to run.

With the spark plugs out, fill the engine with oil; crank the engine until the oil pressure comes up. If you don't have any oil leaks, put the spark plugs back in and hook up the water-cooled radiator and start it up.

After all of this work, the engine sounds like music to the old car enthusiast.

Opposite top: **This is the left side of the Franklin engine. I have added a full flow oil filter and alternator.** *Bottom:* **This is the right side of the engine where I installed a coil so that I could run the engine on the stand.**

CHAPTER 6

The Chassis

The car needs to be stripped down to just the frame and axles, but at some time in this project we will start putting it back together. But before we do even that, the springs and axles will have to be removed. Clean the frame with a scraper and a wire brush and then sandblast it if you have a sandblaster. Check for any cracks and loose rivets and weld them where necessary.

My Franklin's frame looked okay, so I painted it with rust-inhibitor paint and then I primed and painted it black. With the frame ready, I know have a foundation to start putting this car back together.

I took the springs apart to clean the rust off and to replace the center bolts. In the case of the Franklin, I had eight springs to clean up and for which I had to check the arch.

You can take your springs to a spring shop and have them re-arched or you can do it yourself. I compared the upper and lower spring leaves of each side of the front and then the upper and lower ones of each side of the back with each other. For the spring leaf with the most arch, I hammered its corresponding opposite spring leaf to match. My thinking is that the spring wouldn't arch more through the years, but flatten out. After matching all the leaves, I then bolted the springs back together so that they would end up with close to the same amount of arch.

On assembling the Franklin springs, I had to shift some of the leaves from one spring to the other of the pair in order to get the arch close to matching. I then measured the upper and lower springs

I am down to the bare frame. The only parts left are riveted in place.

and put the sets together in a way to come up with the same total arch for each side.

If one semi-elliptic spring has more arch (¼-inch or less) than the opposite side, put the spring with the most arch on the right side of the car to compensate, because, when you drive, the crown in the road tends to tilt a car to the right and consequently causes some weight shift. Engine torque also adds to the weight shift.

There are Teflon strips you can obtain to put between the leaves. I would use them if I had semi-elliptic springs, at least on the two or three longest leaves. The Franklin with full elliptic springs rides well anyway, but if I am not satisfied, the Teflon strips are something that can be done later.

The front axle is a pretty dependable component of the car. Just look at the chassis before removing it to see if it looks bent and that the camber isn't way out of specs. Cars of this era still used solid axles with quite a bit of positive camber (where the wheels lean out at the top). If both sides are the same, you are probably okay. Shake the wheel sideways to check any play in the kingpins. If you have some play, make sure that it is not the wheel bearings by looking for move-

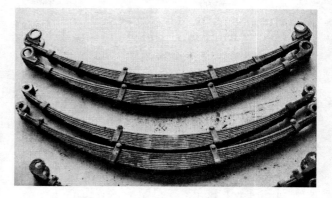

This is the upper and lower rear springs before I took them apart and cleaned them.

ment between the spindle and the hub. Worn pins and bushings can be replaced and are available for most cars. I couldn't find any of those for my 1928 Dodge, so I made some out of drill rod (tool steel) that is a tough steel, but still machinable. I made the bushings out of brass stock, but whether you make or buy them, you will have to ream the bushings after they are installed, as they are a press fit and the diameter decreases when pressed in.

I was lucky again with the Franklin, as the kingpin and bushings were in good shape.

The thrust bearings are readily available at any bearing supply; ask for the bearing number rather than for a part for the make and model of car that you are working on. Bearings of the same number work the same, no matter what the applications.

You probably will find that the tie rod is bent; at least in my experience it is usually bent to more or less some degree. It is no big deal — just remove it and, with a heavy mallet and a block of wood, beat the bend out. The toe will have to be adjusted, but wait until the car is assembled together with all of the weight on it before making the final adjustment. There are generally two methods used to adjust the tie rod. You can screw the ends, or if the tie rod has left and right threads on opposite ends, screw the tie rod. The other common method used on cars of this era is to shim the ball and socket joints at the end of the tie rod. Don't remove the shims; just shift them to the inside of the socket to make the rod longer, or to the outside to make it shorter. Some engineers must have won a contest for the unhandiest way to adjust the tie rod with this method.

Once you install the tie rod you have to check the toe alignment. Let us say that the wheels are straight and parallel with each other. You want ⅛-inch toe in at the tread. The tie rod is about halfway between the kingpin and the tread, so any adjustment at this point will be doubled at the tread. When you shift a shim, you add to one measurement and subtract from the other.

With this knowledge, I may determine that I need to shift a ⅟₃₂-inch shim from the outside of the socket to the inside. This means, of course, that the tie rod needs to be removed on one end, and the ball removed from the socket, just to move the shim.

The rear axle usually doesn't require much repair when restoring a car, except the seals always leak grease.

Remove the differential cover and wheel hubs and check for any loose or bad bearings. If the bearings on the differential are okay and the gears look okay, then leave well enough alone. Any attempt to adjust the gear lash or bearing load will change the ring-and-pinion-wear pattern and may cause a noisy gear set.

In case you have to change a bearing or make adjustments, get the gear mesh back to where it was as close as is possible. Of course, if the gears are badly worn and out of alignment they will have to be replaced. In replacing the ring and pinion gears with used parts, try to get the whole differential assembly and not just the ring and pinions, as getting the same wear pattern in a different housing is next to impossible.

I like to replace all of the seals with modern neoprene seals. The trick here is to get a seal catalog. Measure the shaft or hub and the bore and find a seal in the catalog that will fit. Remember that the outside of the seal will be .005-inch to .015-inch oversized to give a press fit into the bore, but get the nominal size. Cars of this era used leather or felt seals that, if you can't find a modern replacement, you can make.

I have cut leather seals on my wood lathe. Screw a block of wood to your faceplate and then screw a piece of leather to the block of wood with two screws near the center. With a knife tool cut the outside diameter and then the

Here is a seal retainer that I made to accept a modern seal, replacing the original oil slinger.

inside diameter. I cut at an angle on the inside to produce a knife-edge on the top grain side of the leather. You can make a seal this way as good as the original, which of course isn't saying much.

In order to install a modern neoprene seal in the Franklin, I had to make a new seal retainer for the pinion shaft. The original retainer wasn't of sufficient diameter for me to bore out to fit the new seal. I made one retainer out of aluminum stock about the same shape as the original, but one inch larger in outside diameter, bored it to the nominal outside seal diameter and pressed the seal in place. I installed it on the differential housing and, after it was painted, it looked like the original part.

By the 1930s most cars were using a single disk flat clutch, similar to a modern clutch. The thing to check for here is the condition of the pressure plate and the flywheel. If they are bad, warped or rough (from heat), have the machine shop resurface them; but most of the time I have found them to be in satisfactory shape.

The friction plates of this era were generally just a flat disk with lining riveted to it. There weren't any torsion-damping springs or squeeze springs incorporated. I recommend trying to find a modern friction plate to replace the original. Look for one with the same overall shaft diameter that the original had, the same spline, and whether the hub is flat or dish-shaped.

For example, my Dodge took a ten-inch Ford truck friction plate. It was ⅛-inch too big in overall diameter and so I chucked it in the lathe and ground it down to a 9⅞-inch plate.

With the Franklin, I couldn't find a modern replacement for the friction plate due to the deep dish at the hub. The original does have torsion springs, so I am using that, even though some squeeze springs would make for a smoother operation. The clutch and brake shop relined my original with soft lining, but stay away from the woven lining for a clutch, as it has a tendency to grab.

It is common for your transmission to be in good condition. There isn't too much to go wrong, since synchronizers weren't in use yet, and the low power and speed in the 1930s cars didn't put a lot of strain on the gearbox.

The bearings can be replaced and are readily available at your bearing supply store if you find that they are showing some excessive wear. There is a trick to assembling a transmission with uncaged rolling bearings inside the counter shaft. Put the bearings in place with some grease. Next, make a dummy shaft the same length as the counter shaft and slide it inside. Place the whole thing in the case and push the dead shaft through the case, pushing out the dummy shaft. This way all of your bearings will stay in place.

If you have a transmission with broken gears, it is probably best to look for another. There seems to be more old running gears around than body parts, so it shouldn't be too hard to find another. Also, different makes of cars use the same transmissions.

In the more common cars, like the Model A Ford, new replacement parts are available for almost all of the running gears.

The Franklin used a big heavy Detroit gear transmission. It's older than I am and in better shape, so I just cleaned it up and flushed it out. I then replaced the rear seal with a modern one and painted it and filled it with 90w–140w gear oil. I like to add a pint of STP to the gear oil as it helps it to cling to the gears and bearings.

One of the major wear points of old cars is in the universal joints. The problem is keeping the grease in and dirt out. Of the major brands and types of the era, none seemed to have solved that problem

Some cars, the Franklin included, used a flange-drive connection at the transmission and rear end. I am building a car to drive, so I will have a new driveline made up with modern U joints and flange mount. This way if I want to put the original driveline back, it is just a matter of unbolting the new one and replacing it with the original.

If you want to drive at modern highway speeds, you may want to install an overdrive gearbox behind the transmission. In this case, a new driveline is mandatory.

Road rally rules allow for overdrive, but not higher-ratio ring and pinion, unless the higher ratio was available in that specific model year of the car.

The other common drive shaft is enclosed in a torque tube with only one universal joint at the transmission end. These types, like in the Model A Ford, make it more difficult to install an overdrive, but with some machine work it can be done.

There are some companies that make this kind of drive shaft, which is probably the best kind to get. The torque tube not only takes the torque load of the rear axle, but the thrust also. One would have to factor all of these issues in when attempting to install an overdrive.

The steering gear is a very dependable component of the automobile, but one should check it over when restoring a car. This requires complete disassembly and soaking all of the parts in solvent. After checking all of the gears and bearings over, the problem, if any, is to adjust all of the components in relation to each other. In order to do this, it has to be done in the proper sequence.

I like to adjust each bearing or gear as I assemble the unit. In this way, I know that the drag of load I feel is at the part that I am trying to adjust. Install the worm (Ross-type cam) and adjust the thrust bearing with a slight drag and no endplay. On worm-and-gear, worm-and-sector, or worm-and-roller gears (like with the Franklin), install the cross shaft and adjust the endplay either with a setscrew or shims on the cover.

Next, adjust the gear lash with the gear and sector — or roller — centered on the worm. This is done by an eccentric bolt on the cover or eccentric bushing on the cross shaft. It should have some drag in the center, but free up if the wheel is turned in either direction. With the Ross-type cam and lever, the slack is taken up by shims or set screws moving the lever pins tight into the cam.

After the gearbox is adjusted, fill it with a soft grease. Gear oil tends to leak out around the cross shaft bushings and control rods, as these old steering gears didn't have any seals except those made with felt or leather, which don't seal oil very well. If you have sufficient metal to work with at the end of the cross-shaft bushing, one could counterbore the boss and fit a modern seal in it. I like to do this if possible, and then also put a seal at the lower end of the steering shaft where the control rods come out, if necessary. With these changes, gear oil can be used with better overall results.

We won't be able to adjust the drop arm or drag link until the steering gear is installed back on the chassis. This may have to be done after the body is back on the chassis, or in conjunction with the body installation, depending on the car.

Cars of the 1930s were just coming out with hydraulic brakes. Most makes at the time still were using mechanical systems.

Of the mechanical types, there were generally two systems being used. The "Bendix" type used rods, cables and levers to operate a cam that spread the shoes. The anchor pins for the shoes are mounted near the cam like a modern drum hydraulic brake. The shoe toward the front will be the shorter of the two, as the rotating force tends to push it around, applying force to the back shoe. Therefore, the back shoe does the most braking and receives the most wear. This mechanical principle is called a self-energizing — or servo — brake.

The "Midland" brake used a toggle to force the shoes to the drum. The toggle is a V-shaped link with the brake cable attached at the apex of the V. As the cable is pulled, the V flattens out causing a lateral movement. This brake is also self-energizing as the anchor pin and shoe motion is similar to the "Bendix." The brake adjustment is more critical though, as the shoe movement is variable in relation to the cable travel due to the angle changes in the toggle. Too sharp an angle and there is not enough lateral force; too flat an angle and there is not enough lateral movement. The "Lockheed" hydraulic brakes were of both the external-contacting and the internal-expanding type.

The external (or band-and-drum) brakes are self-energizing, as any band brakes are when moving in one direction. In order to have some braking effect when the car is backing up, the anchor pin is located about ⅔ of the way around the brake band. A hydraulic cylinder working through walking beams at each end pulls the band tight to the drum. The rotating drum tends to pull ⅔ of the band tighter and pushes about ⅓ of it away from the drum. Therefore, the effective brake area is only about ⅔ of the band. (With an early hydraulic band brake, like in the 1924 Moon, the anchor was half of the way around the band.)

The hydraulic internal expanding (shoe-and-drum) brakes are similar to modern-drum type hydraulic brakes except that they aren't self-energizing. The hydraulic cylinder forces the shoe toward the drum, but the anchor pin is at the opposite end of the shoes, so no force from one shoe is transferred to the other. The shoe toward the front is the leading shoe and should be the longer if there is any difference in the two.

The shoe-and-drum brake is the type of system both my Dodge and the Franklin had. In fact, they both used the same type of wheel cylinder. The main difference is that the Dodge had 12-inch drums and the Franklin had 14-inch drums. Also, the master cylinders were different.

In most old cars with hydraulic brakes, the Franklin included, the cylinders will be rusted beyond repair. If you want the car in as original condition as possible, have your cylinders sleeved with stainless steel or brass. I would go for the stainless steel for a little more cost as it will virtually never wear out. The brake lines are copper with banjo-type fittings that are susceptible to leakage. (Since I wanted to restore the Franklin to drive and not necessarily for a show car, safety was more important than originality.)

I purchased a sealed double-master cylinder and new wheel cylinders of the same diameter as the original. With the new cylinders I could use steel brake lines with inverted flare fittings. The sealed system would also be less prone to internal rust.

The new wheel and master cylinder-mounting bolt patterns are different than the original, so I made some adapter plates in order to install them.

There is one more point to help make your brakes better: Make sure that the shoes match the drum. Before putting the shoes onto the axles, check how they fit in the drum. Then slide the shoe around in the drum and look to see just where the contact point is. If there is some brake dust still in the drum, it should leave black spots on the lining. If the drums are cleaned up, then you can use some chalk-line chalk to do the drums. Dust the inside of the drum with the chalk and then slide the shoes around and the lining will pick up the chalk at the high points. With some 80-grit emery cloth and a block, sand off the high spots. I use the belt sander but use some discretion and don't overdo it. Check your progress until you get about eighty percent contact. Keep the shoes and drum together as a set. This will give you good brakes right away and stop the spongy feeling you sometimes get, especially with the pressed steel drums. The break-in time will be greatly reduced.

With the frame, axle and springs all repaired, I could now start putting the car back together.

I put the axle under the frame and installed the springs at this point. I then installed the new wheel brake cylinders and the relined brake shoes.

After repacking the front wheel bearings and replacing the grease seals, I then installed the front hubs and drums, and then I went ahead and put the drums on the rear axle.

I had already sandblasted these components, so it was just a matter of cleaning up any dirt or grease on them and doing the painting.

I like to paint the entire undercarriage with anti-rust paint as it stops the rust and gives a good hard finish. This paint will fade easily though, so any part that is exposed to the sunlight will have to be painted with a regular topcoat. To do this you will have to dust-coat the rust inhibitor paint with primer while it is still tacky, otherwise the primer won't adhere to the anti-rust paint.

I dust-coated, primed and top-coated the complete undercarriage, since I wasn't sure just how much would be exposed to the sun. It was easier than trying to figure out how much to apply and it cost just a little more paint.

I still hadn't cleaned up the wheels or even removed the old tires, so I temporarily installed them back on the axles and rolled the

With the frame and axles painted, the car is now starting to come back together.

chassis assembly back into my shop. I already had the engine rebuilt as I discussed earlier, so I put it back in place.

The clutch was ready to install as I had the friction plate relined and replaced the pilot bearing. The clutch cross shaft was hollow, so I drilled a ⅛-inch hole into the shaft at each bearing point. I then put a pipe plug in one end and a grease zerk in the other and pumped grease through the shaft to lubricate all of the bearing points.

After painting the transmission, I put it back in place.

To meet road rally rules and to have more road speed, I decided to install an overdrive. I had modified a Ford overdrive to fit a Marmon Coupe a couple of years ago and it is still working well, so I decided on this approach. I bought a transmission with an overdrive at a swap meet and took it apart only to discover that it wasn't worth trying to repair.

I then acquired a four-speed pickup transmission with "fourth" being an overdrive. I took it apart and removed all of the gears except third (direct) and fourth. I cut the tail shaft off and cut a keyway in it. I then made a seal and bearing retainer and installed it on the back of the transmission where I had removed the tail shaft housing. I made a flange drive the same dimension as the original ones on the car and installed it on the cut off tail shaft. I then fabricated an adaptor to fit the output-drive flange of the Franklin transmission and the input shaft of my modified four-speed. Next, I installed my overdrive into the chassis using a machinist level and a dial indicator to insure proper alignment.

By shortening the tail shaft, I now had room for about thirty-two inches of driveline. A trip to the junkyard yielded a two-piece driveline out of a Chevy Van. I used the yokes off of the longer piece and made adapters to fit the overdrive transmission and the Franklin rear end. I cut the other piece off about two inches and welded it back together in the lathe, using a dial indicator to make sure that I had it straight. Using the slip joint and two new U joints, I installed my homemade driveline, making sure that I had the yokes lined up.

By removing the overdrive transmission and my drive-flange

adaptors, I could return the car back to the original drive train, with the only changes in the car being six holes in the frame web where I bolted a couple of cross members to hold the overdrive transmission.

With the transmission in place, I could now install the brake and clutch pedal. I mounted the new master cylinder where the original had been and, with a little adjustment, the push rod from the pedal worked fine.

The junkyard also produced a proportioning valve that I mounted to the left of the master cylinder on the frame web.

By looking through the brake-hose catalog at the brake-and-clutch repair shop, I found brake hoses for the front wheels and rear axle. I installed them and proceeded with the brake line plumbing. I use ¼-inch steel line from the master cylinder to the proportioning valve as the fitting dictated and ³⁄₁₆-inch line from the valve to the hoses and also at the rear axle. I ran the brake line where the original copper lines were, using the same retaining brackets at the hose connections. Where the lines were outside the frame at the front wheels, I slid a ¼-inch hose over the line to help keep road gravel from chafing the line. At the rear axle, I used wire-bound line.

The next component to install was the steering gear. As I mentioned before, I checked it over and found it to be okay and therefore I just cleaned it up and painted it. Originally, it was bolted to the frame with ⁵⁄₁₆-inch bolts of questionable grade. Also, the holes were wallowed out. This seemed like an unsatisfactory situation to the untrained eye. Two things about driving are important: to be able to stop and to steer. Steering is much more precise with the gearbox bolted in place.

I drilled out the ⁵⁄₁₆-inch holes to ⅜ inch and used four new grade-8 S.A.E. (Society of Automotive Engineers) bolts with hard washers under both the bolt head and nut. When drilling a hole oversized, as in this case, grind a 0-degree rake on the drill bit; this helps keep it from hogging in.

The original gas tank was rusted out, so a replacement was necessary. I used the old gas tank to make a pattern for the end profile, which I took to the sheet metal shop. They made a tank out of 18-gauge cold rolled steel and welded it with a wire welder. I didn't have the filler neck put in, as I couldn't determine the exact location until I fit the tank into place. After I fit it in, I put a hole in the tank and welded in a filler neck that I obtained from the junkyard.

This car was equipped with a "King Seeley" gas gauge, but it was corroded beyond repair. I found a usable gauge at a swap meet, but it was for a tank of considerably less depth. At the hobby shop, I obtained some brass tubing to extend the gas pickup and the air tubes to make the unit workable.

I bought a two-inch flat washer and brazed it to the top of the tank. This was thick enough that I could drill and tap the five mounting screws of the sending unit. I painted and mounted the

With just the engine back in the chassis and the brakes and gas plumbing in place, the car is drivable.

tank in place and installed a backup electric fuel pump and ran the gas line forward to the engine.

When I connected the fuel hose to the steel line, I made a bead at the end of the steel line. I did this with the flaring tool, stopping after the first step of making a double lap flare. This would prevent the hose and clamp from sliding off of the line.

The chassis is actually drivable at this time. At this point, I installed a battery and hooked up a jumper wire to the coil and started the old girl up. With the rear axle jacked up, I checked out the clutch and gears and everything seemed to work fine.

I ordered a tailor-made exhaust system; when it arrived, I painted it with high-heat paint and installed it.

I took apart and cleaned up the shock absorbers and installed new seals and oil. Next they were painted and put back in the car in the same location as they had been originally.

I had to clean up and paint the bumper brackets at the same time as the shocks because they were mounted with the same bolts.

I held off on clamping the fuel and brake lines in place until I did the electrical wiring. Then I clamped them all at once, making sure that nothing chaffed on the frame or other components.

In order to fill the steering gear with grease, I needed the control rods in place, and before the control rods go in, the steering wheel had to be installed. This is important to do before the body goes back on the chassis, especially if you have an enclosed car. It is a good possibility that there is insufficient room within the car body to install the five-foot long control rods inside the steering column. I have had a few experiences where I have had to unbolt the steering gear and drop arm and then unclamp the steering column under the dash. Then I had had to shift the complete assembly around until I could get the rods out of the column!

If the steering wheel is adjustable (as with the Franklin) lower it as far down as you can before the body goes back on. You won't have to lift it as high to clear the steering wheel, which could prove difficult if you don't have a high ceiling in your shop or garage.

CHAPTER 7

Body Restoration

The chassis is pretty much completed now. The next step is to make some links from the shock-absorber arms to the axles, but first you have to determine the length. To do this the car should be pretty much completed. With the body, fenders, bumpers, etc. all in place, the springs will be compressed to the normal load, and then you can measure the distance. This is critical, as you don't want your shocks to bottom out in either direction.

You still have car parts scattered all around your work place, but the pile should be down to just the body parts by now. With the chassis out of the way, sort out your body parts. All of the major parts that need chrome plating (like the radiator shell and bumpers) take or send to your plating shop.

I have discovered from having parts plated before that you get what you pay for. Check prices and go for the middle range for a car that you are going to drive, like I did with the Franklin. If you are going for a show car, get the best and expect to pay for it. Also, I want to stress how important it is to make a list of all of the parts that you are sending out to be plated. Send one copy of the list with the parts and keep a copy for yourself. When the parts are returned to you, go through your checklist to be sure that you have received them all. The fact that I did this was my saving grace in getting everything back. You may not have a problem, but this will help avoid one.

Next, sort out all of the interior parts like the window frame, dash panel, etc. If these have a wood-grain finish, you may want to

The firewall looks more like a sieve than a firewall. The original holes were punched in. Holes added later were drilled, and I filled all of those.

tackle the job yourself. I know my limitations, so I turned the job over to a friend. In some cars these parts are painted the body color. If so, they can be painted when you do the body. A few cars of this era still had wood window frames that you could make if needed. In this case, I would wait and do the woodwork when doing the upholstery. If you have someone do the wood graining or woodwork for you, get them started at this time, so that you will have the parts when you are ready for them.

Order all of your materials for the body: the top material, window channel, fender welt, running-board mat, etc. It takes awhile to get some of these things, so get the process started. I sent my major parts off to be plated, took the wood grain parts to a friend and I had the metal shop bend me up some new running boards.

The Franklin was going to be two colors, so I sorted the remaining parts accordingly. I piled the fender, kick panel and aprons out behind the shop. I sandblasted the body, doors and hood to prepare them for painting.

The bodywork and paint job is what most people look at when they check your car over. This is also the part of restoring that I least like to do and I don't claim to be an expert at it. I will cover what I did with the Franklin, but if you know a better way of doing this, by all means do it your way. (In fact, on any aspect of the project, don't do it the way that I suggest if you know of a better way.) I am covering what worked for me, but like everyone should be, I am open to better ideas.

This car was originally painted a light blue body with black fenders. I discovered this after removing several layers of paint; so if you want your car to be the same color as it was originally, look for a sample of the original paint that is not faded out or covered up with successive layers of paint. Under trim or door bumpers is a good place to find the original paint.

Paint chips are available for most high-production cars, and with computerized equipment, a good paint shop can mix the exact color.

With many of the low-production cars, like the Franklin, the customer could have a custom paint job usually done at the dealer. Even though most Franklins came from the factory already painted, the fact that custom paint was available means that there isn't a truly correct color for them.

My wife liked the idea of a custom paint job, so she picked out the color for the Franklin. Her choice was burgundy and beige. I would have picked more conservative colors, but after spending this much time and money on the car, I was lucky to still have a wife. It was a pretty small price to pay. With the colors that I was supposed to get circled on the color chart, and my credit card, I headed for the auto paint store.

A beige color is light so I needed two coats. Because this would be for the body, it would take three quarts. For just a little more money I figured I might as well get a gallon. I got a gallon of the burgundy paint for the fenders. I also needed the metal etch primer, the sandable primer, the catalyst, some lacquer filler, body filler, a reducer for each can of paint — I spent just over $500.00 but that is what the credit card is for. I don't have to worry about it for a month.

As I mentioned before, I sandblasted all of the parts I was preparing to paint. With your compressor, air blow all of the sand out of the cracks and crevices; go over every area three or four times (though sometimes sand still appears when you start painting).

Iron out all of the dents that you can as close as possible to the original profile, but no closer.

I had some rust at the bottom of the doors. To repair this, I cut some strips of 18-inch gauge steel. I painted the inside of the doors and the strips with anti-rust paint, slipped the strips between the wood door framing and door skin and then glued them in place. I used some wooden wedges to hold the strips tight to the skin until the paint dried.

The next step was to paint everything with the metal etch paint. The reducer for this stuff is an acid, so be sure to wear a good respirator when spraying it or when spraying any paint for that matter. No paint is good for you, but this stuff will take the hair off of a hog.

The pink putty (or filler) comes next, unless you are a purist and want to use body lead. I used body lead on one car, but it is a lot more work and expense and not important unless you are going for a 100-point show car.

Fill in any low spots and smooth over any rough areas. A semi-stiff plastic scraper works well — even your credit card works as a scraper on small areas. The filler shouldn't be very thick or it will tend to crack over time. Some people don't apply more than ¼-inch thick. I try for about half that much, maximum.

Sand the filler to the correct contour. What worked for me was to use 80-grit flex backcloth abrasive. Finer grit than 80 loaded up too fast. So will the 80 grit after awhile, but since it is flexible, you can clean it by drawing it over the edge of your workbench, abrasive side up. A dry cellulose sponge makes a good sanding block. It is stiff enough to bridge the low spots, yet it can be bent to form a contour.

After you have spread the filler on and sanded it off a few times, touch up any area where you sanded off the metal etch paint. Though you will try to avoid this, it will happen around filled areas.

Spray you sandable primer next. This primer dries fast. In fact it dries in the space between the paint gun nozzle and the part that you are trying to paint. To avoid this, use the high-temperature reducer and thin the primer just enough to be able to spray, and then use the minimum air pressure. If you have a temperature- and humidity-controlled paint booth that will help. I had neither, so I spray painted early in the morning and kept the parts out of the sun.

Dry sand your primer with 280–320-grit paper using a sanding block. The idea here is to fill in the sandblast pits, die scratch and grinding marks. Any low spots show up readily when you sand the primer. You shouldn't have any major areas. If you do, go back to the filler and dab any small areas with the lacquer filler to touch up. Lightly sand any lacquer filler and you are ready to put on a second coat of primer.

Sand the second coat of primer with 400-grit paper, wet if possible. Any part that is small enough to handle should be taken out where you can run water on it as you sand. On the body, I used a sponge and a bucket of water to keep things wet as I worked.

After letting everything dry out for a day or two, you are ready for the color paint. You may think that the primer looks perfect, but when the high-gloss color goes on, all of the mistakes that you didn't even know were there show up. If any area is in doubt, now is the time to fix it, before you paint the color on.

I decided to put the chicken wire on the top at this point. I didn't want to scratch up the paint job putting it on later and, as I mentioned, I was giving the water that had seeped into the body a chance to dry out. I couldn't find any one-inch chicken wire that was six feet wide, so I had to settle for the three-foot wide chicken

I installed the chicken-wire top before painting.

wire. I laced it down the center of the top with stainless-steel safety wire.

Starting at the center in front, I stapled down about six inches of wire, then went to the back and pulled it tight and stapled it down about the same amount. On the middle of one side, I pulled the wire toward me and stapled it down every six inches or so. Then I went to the other side and pulled it tight and stapled it down. Then I worked from the center to the corners from front to back and then left to right alternately, until I reached the corners. I stapled every wire around the perimeter of the top.

I cut the wire through the next opening outside of the staple, then bent it over and tucked it under the opening in the wire just inside where it was stapled. This keeps it from sliding under and making the whole thing loose. I then tucked the loose ends under to prevent them from coming through the top material later.

This is the body after the color paint was applied. I also painted the doors, hood and smaller upper body parts at the same time.

To get a good paint job, you will want a dust-free, humidity-and-temperature controlled room with good lighting. I had none of the above, but gave it my best shot anyway.

Mix your paint as per directions; make enough to do the job, but no more. Once you have added the hardener to the paint, you have to use it and you can't pour any excess back into your paint can or you will ruin whatever paint is left. I sprayed the hard-to-reach areas first, like inside the windshield frame and door header. I was sure to get around the corners at the doorposts, etc. That way I would have some overlap with the upholstery later. Then I started at a break in the body, like a door opening. I worked from the top to the bottom and then to the left (if you are right-handed). This way I could stay out of as much over-spray as possible while holding the air hose out of the way with my left hand. I sprayed enough paint to keep the wet look, but not enough to make it run or sag.

With the parts — like the hood — that I wanted to paint on both sides, I painted the inside first, and then the next day I painted the outside. This way any over-spray wouldn't be on the side that is most noticeable. A better way, if you have the room, is to hang the parts on a wire and spray both sides at the same time.

After the body and related parts were painted, I started with the assembly.

I decided to put the top material on while I had the body sitting on the floor because it was easier to reach.

With the chicken wire already in place, the next material to add to the top was the cotton batting. It is an inch or so thick (you can't measure it with any accuracy) and separates easily to form a layer

I put the cotton padding over the chicken wire and then the top material while the body was still sitting on the shop floor.

half as thick. It took two ½-inch thick strips to cover the top, by laying them side by side; then I laid another strip down the middle on top of the first two. I then separated a vertical strip down the center and put the two half-wide strips on each side of the one in the middle of the car top. This way I had the full 1-inch thick padding, but with the seams staggered.

I trimmed the cotton to fit the top, then padded it down so that it binded together and carefully tapered the edges by pulling off thin layers of cotton. I put a strip of duct tape along each side so I could staple the cotton in place.

This step wouldn't need to be taken with a car with just a top insert, but the top material on the Franklin comes down to the gutters on each side and as I pulled the material down over the wood frame, the cotton wanted to come with it.

The original material for the top of these old cars was a heavy cotton duck with rubberized paint on it. The cotton duck tended to stretch in damp weather and shrink up in dry, causing the rubber paint to form small ridges, especially after it cracked and was repainted several times. The modern replacement is a vinyl-covered cotton duck with the ridges already formed in the vinyl.

My problem was the modern duck only came in 54-inch or smaller width and I needed 68 inches to reach from gutter-to-gutter. What I found was a woven polyester, with a leather-grained vinyl coating on it. It was lighter than the cotton, but stronger, and it came in seven foot-widths. Of course, black would have been my choice, as that was the color of all the car tops in 1930. But my wife, being an artist, didn't care what they used in 1930; black didn't go with the beige body, so a light tan was a close match. There is a practical side to her choice as black and Arizona sun don't go together very well. Well, one has to find some solace in losing...

When choosing a vinyl top material, make sure that it is a woven backing and not a knit. When the vinyl gets warm in the sun, the knit stretches like a cheap sweater.

The top material in stalls best when it is warmed up; if it is a cotton-back vinyl, a little moisture on the backing won't hurt. Park your car in the sun and roll the top material out and let it set for awhile. I didn't have the body on the chassis at the time, so I couldn't move it out into the sun, but it was plenty warm in the Arizona summer anyway.

I stapled the top material down working end-to-end, and side-to-side like I did with the chicken wire installation. But be sure that the trim molding will cover where you have stapled.

I trimmed and rolled the top material under on the sides of the Franklin to give a finished edge that was even with the door header; that way the gutter covered the staples.

I installed the trim molding at the front and back of the top material. I used stainless steel screws in the bottom of the channel because it is about impossible to pull a nail out of a channel. This is in case I have to replace the top later on and want to get it off without ruining the molding.

One idea that worked well was to put masking tape about 1/16-inch from where the trim molding goes, then spread the caulking and press the molding into it and then fasten it down. The excess caulking will squeeze out onto the masking tape. I could then wipe the caulking off of the molding with a rag dampened with acetone. The acetone isn't too good for the vinyl, but with the molding clean I could just pull off the masking tape and have a neat-looking job.

The gutter had an anchor strip that I screwed on with stainless steel flathead screws about every two inches. The gutter is supposed to slide on the anchor strip, but with the curve of the body, it didn't want to slide very easily. So I lubricated the anchor strip and gutter with liquid dish soap and, with my air hammer, drove the gutter on in just about ten seconds. I trimmed the gutter to length after it was in place, as the air hammer flattened the end out pretty bad.

I was ready to put the body on the chassis, when I remembered that the rear apron had to go on first. I wanted everything below the body floor to be a burgundy color, so I had to clean the apron up and go through the steps to get it painted. I also painted the rear

This is the body back on the chassis with the windshield, sun visor and tire mounts back in place.

wheel wells at this time as I was going to paint the fenders on both sides.

With that painting job done, I then backed the chassis into the shop, raised the body up with a couple of come-alongs, rolled the chassis under it and let it down in place.

At this stage of the project I began to get excited, or at least as excited as I ever get. After all of these months, it was beginning to look like a car again. The object is to get all of these car parts back into one pile — putting the body back on the chassis was a big step in that direction.

Between the body and the body mounts on the chassis, I used a strip of body webbing typical of cars of this era. The object of the webbing was to provide some cushioning effect and help cut down on squeaking. After torquing down the body mount bolts — which put a squeeze on the webbing — I found out that I had to make some shim adjustments to get the body-floor sill even with the frame rails. Once done, I fastened the steering column to the body and replaced the clutch and brake pedals.

I ran all of the wiring for the tail and brake lights down the frame rail. With the fuel and brake line and wiring in place, I clamped everything so the parts don't chafe on the frame or each other. This may seem a minor thing, but securing each system properly will help prevent a major breakdown, or worse, later.

I made all new floorboards using the old ones for patterns but using the same material, in this case ½-inch and ¾-inch plywood. I used a mixture of black paint and linseed oil and painted the floorboards, the oil also waterproofing them to some degree.

I sandblasted and then used rust-preventing paint on the metal parts of the floorboards and floor pan that went between the seats.

While the paint on the floorboards and pan was drying, I hung the doors on the body. I had saved some of the shims that I used when I originally fit the doors, so the installation was pretty simple with just a few minor adjustments. The doors didn't fit perfectly, but I doubt if they ever did because they were wood-framed with a metal skin.

I cleaned up, repaired and then installed the door latch mechanism. I marked them so I could match them back on the same door. With the door latch in place, I could now install the striker plates. I had to find the exact location before I drilled the screw holes, as I didn't want to mess up the doorpost at this stage of the game.

The door being a "wet panel" (meaning the rain water flows down the glass, then inside the door and out the drain holes) I caulked between the door skin and the wood frame. I then insulated the doors (mostly for sound deadening) with closed-cell foam.

To glue something like foam in place, I used contact cement (but as everyone who has used the stuff knows, the key word here is "contact!") Paint the glue on both surfaces to be joined and let it dry to touch. Avoid any contact between these surfaces until you are ready to put them together. In order to slide the foam in the doors behind the gussets, I put a piece of plastic (like a carpet runner) in

Here closed-cell foam is installed inside the doors. The stick holds the window up until I get the window lift installed.

first. Then I positioned my foam and carefully slid the plastic out. Once the foam and door make contact, it is hard to get the foam off. I insulated the rest of the car body with the foam, except for the firewall for which I used foil-back fiber.

I had new safety glass cut for all of the windows using the old glass for patterns. I cleaned up the window-lift mechanism and the glass-setting channel. I pressed the channel onto the glass using glass-setting tape of the correct thickness. This isn't difficult; just make sure that your glass is resting on some padding or your work-bench. Stand it on edge, bottom-side up and place the tape along the glass. Then you press the channel over it. With a mallet, care-fully drive the channel down in place. Trim off the excess setting tape. That step is completed.

With glass-setting rubber and the seal attached, you cannot

install it as described above because the rubber won't slide into the channel evenly and the window seal will be crooked. In this case, place the rubber in the channel, lubricate it with soapy water and slide the glass in from one end of the channel. Make sure that the glass is at the bottom of the channel. The rubber will stretch some as you push the glass through, which will pull the sealed edge tight, giving you a neat, straight seal.

In installing new window channels in the doors, make sure that you don't have any metal fasteners in the glass travel area. Fasten the channel at the bottom below the glass and, if needed, at the very top within the corner radius. Any fasteners that contact the edge of the glass will, over time, cause the glass to crack. It is best to glue the channel with weather-strip adhesive.

Lubricate the window lift gears and the slide area in the lift channel with grease. Install the doors and check the travel. The glass should seal at the top; the seal at the lift channel should make contact at the same time. The door glass should be flush or a little lower than the windowsill when down. On doors like the rear ones on the Franklin, the windows won't retract all the way down due to the cut out for the rear fender. A person couldn't rest their arm on the windowsill anyway due to the seat location.

Next, I set the windshield in its frame with window-set tape. I had to use bar clamps to pull it together, but if one uses discretion, you can put a lot of force on glass edgewise.

One point of interest is that the seal

This is the right-hand taillight bracket that I made using the left bracket for a pattern and reversing the angles. I used 1-inch water pipe and ¼-inch steel plate.

over the windshield hinge is just a strip of top material that wraps over the outside of the hinge. It is held in place with the screws that hold both the hinge on the windshield and the header in the car body. The trick is to have it tight with the hinge closed, but the hinge has to be open to get the screws in. I solved this problem by screwing the seal down with the hinge on the windshield frame; then I closed the hinge, put a strip of double-stick tape on the hinge and pulled the seal tight and stuck it to the tape. I then could open the hinge and screw it to the windshield header and maintain the correct seal placement.

(Note: be sure to install the windshield before you install the sun visor on cars with an outside sun visor like the Franklin had. If the sun visor is in place, the windshield won't open enough to get easy access to the hinge screws.)

With the windshield in place, I now installed the sun visor with a strip of fender welt placed between the sun visor and the body. If you use fender welt, (which cars up to the 1950s do) get the vinyl-covered fabric, not the plastic stuff. The plastic tends to slip out when the parts are drawn together.

Now I was still waiting for my chrome work to come back from the plater but I did what I could without it. I decided to start on the burgundy parts. I needed a right-hand taillight bracket. Cars of this era usually didn't have a right-hand taillight; if they did, it was generally an optional item. Since I couldn't find such a bracket, I made one using the left-hand taillight bracket for a pattern. I took a piece of one inch black pipe, which is about 1¼-inches in its outside diameter, and turned it down on the lathe to match the diameter of the left taillight bracket. I then cut V notches in it to get the sharp bends that I needed. I made the end pieces out of ¼-inch steel plate and brazed the whole thing together using a die grinder with a carbide rasp; that gave it the final shape.

I cleaned up and repaired the kick panels and hood flashing. I had already repaired the shutters so I painted these parts along with the head and taillight brackets.

I installed the floorboards and pan that had been lying around for a week or so and then installed the flashing that goes around the hood area and the headlight and taillight brackets.

I had new running boards made at a sheet metal shop, using the old ones for a pattern. I painted them with anti-rust paint and glued the rubber mat to them with contact cement. (The critical thing to watch for here is to keep the ribs of the matting parallel with the edge of the running board.) I then put new molding around the running boards and installed them with the kick panels. I wouldn't be able to secure them completely until the fenders were installed.

I decided that I would sandblast the last parts that I hadn't cleaned up yet. The only things that were left were the fenders and the front-seat frame.

I had new running boards made at a sheet metal shop. I then painted them and installed the rubber mat and trim. From left to right, the original running boards top and bottom, the new ones showing bottom and top.

The Franklin seat was supposed to be adjustable fore and aft, but it was rusted in place. I took the seat frame apart and sandblasted it to clean off the rust and painted it with anti-rust paint. I lubricated the slide and locking pin and put it in the car.

I was ready to start to work on the fenders which weren't in too bad shape, except for the right rear. It looked like someone rubbed a guardrail once back in the 1940s. They had pounded it back to a reasonable, but rough, contour. All the fenders needed the wire beads welded and some battle scars removed.

I pounded the dents out of the fenders to a reasonable shape with a hammer and a dolly. I then brazed up the cracks and the wire-bead edge of each fender.

For brazing I like to use brass to keep the heat in and therefore the stress out of metal. (I discovered this while working on heavy equipment where a common breakdown happened when the steel hydraulic lines would fatigue and crack. With welding, they would crack along the weld, but with brazing, they would last a long time.) It does take about twice the thickness of brass to get enough strength, though.

The right rear fender was stretched back about four inches due to the aforementioned guardrail grazing. I made a template using the left fender for a pattern. I employed the heat-and-cool method to shrink the bead edge back as close as I could get to the original contour.

Metal that is restrained within a bore or hole — like a bearing race, bushing, pipe plug or bolt — can be removed easily by heating and letting it cool. Heat a small area as fast as possible to a bright red. The metal can't expand due to being restrained, so the area you heat gets thicker, which in fact, displaces some metal. After it has cooled, the part will be loose in the bore due to the metal being displaced.

This trick will also work on something like the edge of a fender, but using a little different technique. Heat one small area on the edge quickly, and then pour water on it to cool it. The metal is not restrained, the heat will even out in time, and you won't displace much metal. By cooling it quickly, initial displacement is preserved before the metal has a chance to even it out. By doing this every inch or two along the bead edge, I shrunk it back almost the full four inches. I now put on a coat of the metal etch paint and proceeded with some body filler to smooth out my hammer work.

Use any filler sparingly on fenders or any part that is subjected to a lot of flex and vibration. I used a little just to smooth out my dent removal, a skill which, I am the first to admit, leaves something to be desired. By covering small areas not very thickly, the filler should last a long time. I also used aircraft filler, which is lighter and more flexible; the disadvantage with that is that it takes about twelve hours to set up. After filling and sanding, prime and paint like any other part of the body. I painted both sides of the fenders, but didn't bother with fillers and sanding the underside. I just primed and lightly sanded to flatten down any irregularities in the primer. Then I painted the underside first, making sure to cover all around the bead edge. This is important, because if you try to cover the edge while painting the upper side, you will get over-side spray on your underside paint.

Now was the time to install the fender welt. Because the Franklin had a wood-framed body, I just tacked the welt either to the body or wheel well, whichever had a definite corner or line to follow. Once you have the fender bolted in place, the welt won't shift about. Trying to bolt the fender and hold the welt in place at the same time will prove to be a bit difficult.

I had to use a double-stick tape to hold the welt in place, while installing the front fenders on the Franklin, as there wasn't any place to tack the welt except a short area at the base of the cowl. There is nothing high-tech about installing fender welts; about the only thing to keep in mind is to clip the web of the welt on corners that bend toward the bead and cut V-notches in the web when bending away from the beaded edge.

The next step is to bolt the fender on. To gain easy access to the bolts, I removed all of the wheels from the car. I decided it was a good time to get the old wheels ready to paint.

The car is almost all back together. All I need is the bright work to come back from the plater.

The rear fenders had oversized oval-bolt holes so as to give plenty of adjustment for correct alignment. I had to rotate the fenders a little to align them with the running board. Then I shifted the running boards in or out as needed so that the running-board molding and fender edges were even. I used new fender washers and bent them to fit the contour of the fender well.

On the front fender, I had to remove the bolts that hold the front shock and bumper bracket in place, because the fender flange slides behind them. The fender braces bolt directly to the frame with no room for adjustment. The only alignment on the front fender is with the running boards, which I bolted together.

I had set the trunk on the brackets to check for fit; that seemed to be okay. I bought the trunk, which was supposed to be for a 1929 Franklin, but it fit the 1930 model. I made a trunk platform out of

wood and covered it with vinyl car-top material, with a little
padding under it. I bolted the platform to the brackets and then the
trunk to the platform.

This car was also equipped with an auxiliary trunk rack, so that
you could carry an extra trunk. I had to clean it up and paint it
while doing the bumper brackets. The trunk-rack brackets bolted on
with the rear bumper brackets, so at this time I bolted them
together. I had some difficulty finding the kind of oval-head ⅜-inch
bolts that were originally used to bolt the rack to the brackets. What
I did find were stainless steel, so I polished the heads and left them
natural. I had some chrome trim to go on the rack, but that had to
wait, like when I got it back from the plating shop.

After a few telephone calls, I finally received my bright work
back from the plating shop. They did a good job on the brass parts
and the white metal, but the steel parts were as poor a plating job as I

Here, the extra folding trunk rack is back in place.

had ever seen. But I was glad to get the parts back! It had taken so long, I was afraid that I would never see them again.

With the shutter assembly repaired and painted, I installed it into the radiator shell along with the screen. The complete assembly was then put on the car.

Next, I riveted the hood hinge to the top-hood panels with pop rivets. It was originally riveted with hollow rivets, but I didn't have the tools to set them. I drove the hinge pin in after the halves were riveted. Next, I put the top part of the hood on the car. Then, I put the hood latch pins on the side panels and slid the hinge pin in place, which holds the side panels to the top of the hood. With the headlights and fender lights in place, I finished the wiring.

Then I installed the rest of the exterior chromed parts, like the bumpers and door handles. The lock shop provided me with a door-key lock for an American Motors car. With just a little modification, I made it fit the Franklin.

CHAPTER 8

The Electrical System

The electrical systems on these old cars are quite simple, so it is not difficult to wire the car, even without a schematic. They are usually not equipped with any safety devices like fuses. The Franklin had a couple of fuses, but most of the circuits were unprotected.

There are several outfits that make up new wire looms for old cars using the original type of wire. These looms are quite expensive, but for a show car, you will need them for that original look.

As I have stated before, I am restoring this car to drive, which includes adding turn signals, an alternator and a few other changes from the original to make it safer and more dependable. Since it is not going to be restored to its original condition anyway, I couldn't justify paying extra for the old cotton-braid lacquered wire they had used originally, when the modern plastic insulation is better. I also didn't want the thing to burn up, so I put a fuse in every circuit and a fusible link in the main hot wire. I also incorporated a battery cut-off switch for safety when the car is stored for a period of time.

One of the first things that you need to determine for the electrical system is which battery post goes to ground. I checked in my handbook for the 1929 models. It listed eighty-two makes and models for that year. Forty-two of them were positive ground or just over half. In scientific thinking, electricity flows from negative to positive. As far as automobiles are concerned, I can't see if it makes any difference, as the circuit has to be completed for the current to flow anyway. The engineers of the time hadn't reached a consensus on the subject either, judging by the fact that just over half of the cars were positive ground.

My Franklin was positive ground, but I installed a negative ground alternator on the car. The only change that I needed to make was switching the battery cable, making it a negative ground. I then switched the wires on the amp meter so that it would read correctly and changed the coil wires so the negative wire would go to the breaker points.

There are only three or four electrical circuits on the car, depending on how you break it down. When you buy a pre-made wire loom, you can order the lighting loom, ignition loom or the starting circuit loom.

If you are wiring your own car from scratch, you can proceed one circuit at a time. I will try to explain each step, using a negative ground system. If you have a positive ground system, just substitute positive for negative in the instructions.

First, you will need three battery cables. One will go from the battery to the ground, usually in the car frame. Second will be a cable from the battery to the starter switch and third, from the switch to the starter. The starter switch is a high ampere switch, usually located on the toe board of the car. (On that Marmon that I helped restore you had to pull up on the horn button for the starter switch.) It is hard to buy battery cables of ten-gauge wire at your auto parts store. Check with the shops that cater to heavy trucks or you can make your own using welding lead.

Run a ten-gauge wire from the battery side of the starter switch to the amp meter, and then a ten-gauge wire from the amp meter to the generator cutout, which is usually mounted on the generator. The cutout connects to the armature of the generator. If you have a regulator in the charging circuit, you will need a couple of more wires.

The voltage regulator terminals are marked, or should be, as A, B, F and sometimes G. One ten-gauge wire goes from your amp meter to the B (battery) terminal. Another ten-gauge wire goes from A (armature) to the generator. Then a 14-gauge wire goes from the F (field) terminal to the field wire on the generator. The G — or ground — wire just grounds the regulator if it is needed. This covers the starting and charging systems.

The ignition circuit is a 14-gauge wire from the battery side of the amp meter to the ignition switch. Then the same size wire goes to the positive side of the coil. If you have a resistor, the wire goes to the resistor and then to the coil. Another 14-gauge wire goes from the negative side of the coil to the breaker points. The high-tension wiring completes the ignition circuit that goes from the coil to the distributor and then to each spark plug.

The lighting is wired by running a 14-gauge wire from the generator side of the ampere gauge to a fuse or terminal block. Then it goes from the block to the light switch. The light switch on my Franklin would have three positions: off, parking or running lights (I never used this position as I didn't know if it meant drive the car or park it), and the headlights. A 14-gauge wire goes from the parking light terminal to the cowl or fender lights. Another 14-gauge wire goes from the headlight terminal to a dimmer switch and then to the taillights. From the dimmer switch, run two 14-gauge wires to the headlights: one is for high beam and one is for low beam. For the dome light, a wire will go from the terminal block to the door switch and then to the dome light. The manual dome light switch is then wired the same as the door switch.

The horn is wired with 12-gauge wire from the terminal block to the horn motor. A wire to the horn button grounds the horn motor. If you use a relay switch, run the wire to the relay and then to the horn. Ground the horn motor and then run the trigger wire from the relay to the horn button.

A 14-gauge wire from the terminal block to the brake light switch, that is actuated by the brake pedal, wires the brake lights. Then run a wire from the brake light switch to the brake lights.

This covers the basic wiring in cars of the 1930s vintage. You may get by with a lighter gauge wire than I suggested, but for a few cents more, I like to use the heavier wire. You may add a few more circuits, such as the cigar lighter, backup lights or an electric fuel pump.

Now, getting back to the Franklin: I had already run the wires to the rear of the car for the tail and stop lights. I put in an auxiliary

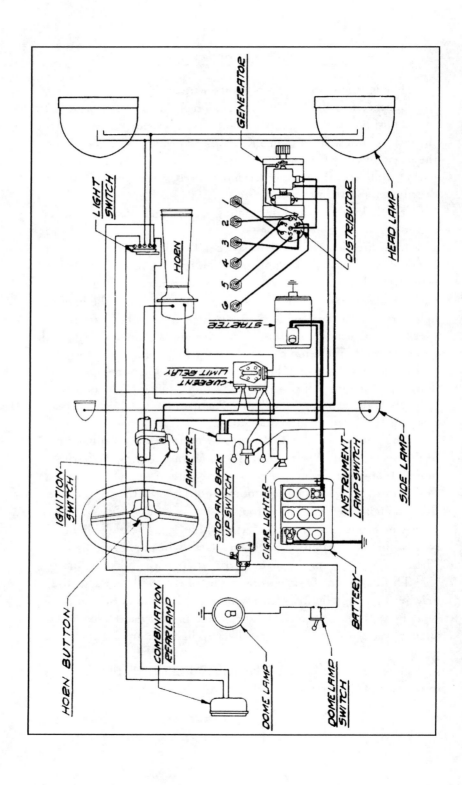

electric fuel pump near the gas tank, so I ran the wires there also. Some cars have an electric gas gauge, so you will need a wire for that. This usually takes care of all of the electric components at the rear of the car.

After installing the fender and headlight mounts, I ran the wires for the respective lights. Since I am also using the fender lights for the turn signals, I ran two wires to each of them.

The original fender-light wire was of the wire-bound type for more protection from the elements. They run under the fender and are subject to debris thrown up by the tires. In order to protect these wires, I made a conduit from a ¼-inch tubing bending it to fit under the fender. I also flared the tubes at each end to avoid chafing the insulation. All of the rest of the wires I ran through braided fabric loom.

I used a one-wire alternator so that I could install the original generator at any time in the future without changing the wiring. The original generator was made before voltage regulators were used on most cars. You could adjust the generator output by moving the third brush within the generator.

When installing turn signals on a car that wasn't originally equipped with them, there are two types of turn-signal control. Use the 7-wire control if you are going to also use your stoplights as rear turn signals. If you are using separate lights for the turn signals, then the 4-wire control will work.

With the 7-wire system you will need to install a right-side tail- and stoplight if your car doesn't have one. These were an option on some makes like the Franklin, but others didn't even offer them. I found a taillight similar to the one on the left side and mounted that.

Next, run the wire from the fuse block through the brake-light switch, then to the signal control. The brake lights will work normally unless the turn signal is on, which will interrupt the circuits

Opposite: **This is a wiring diagram from a 1928 Buick owner's manual, close to what I have just described.**

either on the right or on the left and cause the stop light on that respective side to blink.

Installation directions will come with a new turn signal control, but if you don't have them, it is easy to figure out the seven-wire system: one wire from the brake light switch, two wires to and from the flasher and a wire to each of the four lights in the system.

The four-wire system is much simpler as the brake-light circuit doesn't pass through the signal control. Here the circuit goes through the flasher and then to the signal switch. The front and rear bulbs on each side are on the same circuit. The fourth wire goes from the flasher to the indicator light.

CHAPTER 9

Wheels and Tires

My original plan was to have the wire-spoke wheels stripped of the old paint and rust by the dipping process. I didn't want to sandblast them because if the operator doesn't use a little discretion, he will blast away the spokes. After spending some time on the phone, I discovered that there wasn't anyone around the area that had a dip tank, so I went to Plan B, which was to clean them up by hand.

The wheels were in pretty good shape, with just one coat on paint on them. About the only rust was around the rim where the paint was knocked off in the removing and replacing of the lock ring. I cleaned this area with the disk sander. The rest of the wheel I cleaned by hand. I didn't remove all of the old paint, just where it looked like it may have come loose or had rust blisters.

I touched up any bare metal with anti-rust paint and then I primed and painted the wheels. I have painted wire-spoke wheels before with good results (like on a Model A Ford which only has thirty spokes) by laying them flat and spraying one side and then turning them over and spraying the other side. But since the Franklin wire-spoke wheel had seventy spokes on it, it was going to be impossible to cover all of the area between all of the spokes this way.

I finally came up with the technique of standing the wheel on edge and spraying down on every area that I could see on the front side. Then I rotated the wheel about sixty degrees and did the same thing until I covered the entire wheel. I did the same on the backside and then I laid the wheel flat, front side down, and touched up the bead area. I didn't worry about the front of the hub, since the hubcap covered this part of the wheel.

This era of car makes had three styles of wheels: wood-spoke, wire-spoke and disk. They came in three types: a split rim that was found mostly on wood spoke and disk and the lock ring, found on wire-spoke wheels. The lock ring could be a single or double ring, or it could be a drop-center wheel. I want to cover some repair on the wood-spoke wheels first, as they were the most common type.

In restoring the wood spokes, the old finish should be removed with stripper; sand-blasting would eat away the wood. After the old finish is removed, check to see if any spokes are loose. If none are, then boil your wheel about an hour in linseed oil. (A cut-off 55-gallon drum works well for this purpose.) Wipe the excess oil off the metal parts before they dry and leave the spokes to soak up what

These are a couple of wood spoke wheels from a 1928 Dodge, ready to boil in the linseed oil.

they can. The oil makes a good natural finish, but you can paint over it, too.

With a few loose spokes you can spread the lagging and put a C-shaped shim between the end of the spoke and the lagging, though you may not want to shim a loose spoke. Check the wheel for roundness by measuring between the hub and the lagging. A pair of inside calipers or a dial indicator works well for this. Shim any short spokes no more than .005 of an inch at a time. As you shim the short spokes, the long ones will get shorter and usually by the time you get your wheel round, all of the spokes will be tight.

If you have an original spoke-jack, you can use it to force the lagging out from the hub, or make one out of a threaded rod and long nut. A spreading clamp will also do the job.

If you have a lot of loose spokes, it is best to remove them all and check each one over to see why. They may be worn too much to save because of their running loose for too long.

When removing the spokes, be sure to mark the hub, lagging and spokes so that all parts can be put back to their original position.

Remove the nuts from the hub bolts inside the brake drum. These are usually riveted down in order to lock the nuts on. Slide the hub out of the center of the spokes and lift the spokes out, hub end first.

Check them over and if they are not rotten, broken or worn out, you can probably get by with a shim on the end of each spoke. It doesn't take much to tighten your wheels — just .010 of an inch would take up a lot of slack. Cut a washer-shaped shim and slip it over the trunnion at the lagging end of the spoke. Put the spokes back in order, but raise the center up like a tepee. Then push all of the spokes down flat within the lagging at the same time. They should be tight enough to snap in as they flatten out.

Replace the hub and drum and check for roundness. The closer to perfect, the better it will be. You should get within .020 of an inch at least. If they are out of round too much, move some shims around and when you are satisfied, boil your wheel in the oil and proceed from there. If the wood spokes are in bad shape, it is best to send your wheels to a shop that specializes in rebuilding wood-spoke wheels, or buy some others.

Wire-spoke wheels don't leave the hobbyist much choice when it comes to repair. On the less-expensive cars, they are usually welded spokes and there is no way to make any adjustment. It is quite common for these wheels to be bent, but they can be straightened with a bit of work. You will need to clamp the hub solidly and press the rim into alignment and that requires a more considerable amount of equipment than most amateur restorers have. The other type of wire spokes are the spoke and nipple that can be adjusted, but most of the time the nipple is rusted to the spoke. I would suggest for convenience and safety that you send your wheels to a shop that specializes in wheel repair.

The Franklin had spoke- and nipple-wire wheels, with a single lock-ring for removing and replacing the tires. Any wheel needs to be designed in a way to facilitate tire replacement. If the split-rim type is forced within itself to make a smaller diameter, it can be inserted inside of the tire then spread back into shape. There is a locking device to lock the ends of the rim together. The advantage of this type is that they are light in weight and the tire can't some off with a loss of air pressure. The disadvantage is that it takes some effort to spring the wheel within itself.

Drop-center wheels, the type that modern cars use, are the simplest and the strongest, since they are one solid piece.

A good example of a lock-ring type wheel from the Franklin.

The tire is forced down into the center of the rim, which will give enough slack to pry the bead off of the rim on the opposite side. Always remove the tire from the front or back of the wheel, depending on which rim edge is closest to the drop center. If the drop is in the center of the wheel, take the tire off of the back of the wheel. You will avoid chipping the paint where it is more noticeable. The disadvantage of this type of wheel is that the tire can come off with a loss of air pressure.

The lock-ring types are probably the easiest to have for changing a tire, but are considered unsafe. I have changed a lot of truck tires with this type of wheel and I never did have a lock ring come off, but you have to pay attention to what you are doing and be sure to use the right lock ring for the wheel, as there are a lot of different designs.

This is my Model A Ford before I restored it back in 1959. Notice the 21-inch drop center wheel on the left front and a 19-inch drop center wheel in the back.

At this point in the restoration, the Franklin wheels were ready to have the tires mounted on them. I had bought four new tires, plus tubes and flaps. This car had room for six wheels, including two spares, but I couldn't see getting six brand new tires because they would just dry out in the Arizona sun. I would have to drive the others a long time just to wear out the four tires on the ground, let alone rotating the two spares in. I picked the best two old tire tubes and flaps for spares and made covers for them so their appearance didn't make that much difference.

I will attempt to explain how to mount a tire. This may seem elementary, but most of us today don't change tires, let alone tires with tubes and flaps. First, get some talcum powder (baby powder works fine) and dust the inside of the tire. (Powdered soap stone can also be used.) Air your tube up enough to hold its shape and dust it with the powder. Now press the tube into the tire. It should be somewhat loose in the tire without any wrinkles. Tuck the flap after dusting in between the tire and the tube and then slide your hand around between the flap and the tire to make sure that the flap is centered between the tire beads with no folds in it.

On a lock-ring wheel, place the tire, tube and flap assembly over the wheel, start the valve stem through the hole in the wheel and drop the tire into place. The trick in putting the lock ring on is to do it without taking the paint off. Spiral the lock ring like a lock washer. Start the un-notched end into the wheel groove. Pry the lock ring over the edge of the wheel starting at about 160 degrees from the split. Push about 90 degrees of the ring into place and advance the pry by about 90 degrees and push the ring down again until you are around to the notch in the lock ring. Pry the last 90 degrees in place by prying in the notch, and then the ring should snap into place. Put enough air in the tube to just push the tire against the lock ring and bead on the backside. If the lock ring isn't tight to the wheel all of the way around, tap it into place with a block of wood and a hammer. If the lock ring looks good, air the tire to the recommended pressure. If you don't have a cage to put it in, then you can air it up from the backside.

In the foreground is a split rim wheel from the Dodge. Just behind me is my partner on the Great American Race, Glenn Crofutt. This photograph was taken by Shirlee Crofutt.

If the lock ring doesn't fit right, let the air out and check to see if there is something keeping it from seating into place. If you have checked the groove and it still doesn't fit into place, don't use it. It is either sprung out of shape, or else it is the wrong lock ring.

With split rims, proceed as above, except you will have to spring the wheel inside of itself and drop it into the tire, then snap it back to its original shape and lock the split together.

With my Dodge, I made a lever with two pins that matched the holes in the rim bead. I put the pins into the holes and swung the lever about 180 degrees, which is like handling a loaded spring. I carefully put it into the tire and moved the lever back to where I started.

With wire-spoke, drop-center wheels, you don't need a flap, but put a rim strip over the end of the spokes so that the tube doesn't chafe on them.

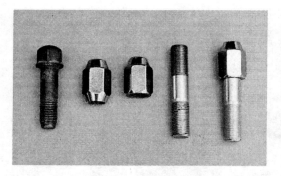

From left to right are an original lug bolt, a chromed lug nut and a nut after being drilled and tapped. I then cut a square on the end. Also a stud made from a bolt, and then the nut and stud screwed together, making a new lug bolt.

With all of my tires mounted, I put the new hubcaps onto the wheels. The lugs are on the outside of the hub and not under the cap. The inner piece of the hubcap crimps to the inside of the wheel hub. The outer part I then glued to the inner with caulking.

The original was a press fit with blotter paper between the inner and the outer parts of the hubcap. Needless to say, they didn't stay on very well. I should have balanced my wheels and tires before installing the hubcaps, because a person can't see the bubble on the balancer with the hubcap in place.

I couldn't buy any original lug bolts for the wheels, and I only had half of what I needed. Each wheel needs seven of them, so I bought twenty-eight, ⁹⁄₁₆-inch bolts and sawed the heads off. Then I threaded the end without the threads. That gave me a stud with fine threads on each end. I then bought twenty-eight chromed ½-inch lug nuts. I drilled and tapped them to a ⁹⁄₁₆-inch and cut the tapered seat off square. I locked the nuts to the studs with a thread lock and ended with a chrome-head lug bolt. It was cheaper than getting my old ones plated, even if I had had enough of them.

CHAPTER 10

The Interior and Upholstery

At this point, the car is about finished except for the interior. I put in the upholstery first and then installed the window frames, door handles, etc.

In preparation for the upholstery work on the Franklin, I got out the old sewing machine. It hadn't been used in years, so I oiled it up and made some adjustments and sewed up some spare tire covers out of vinyl material. I didn't do as neat a job as I would have liked, but by the time I was finished, I had the sewing machine working pretty well. The material was inexpensive and it was good practice for me before I got started on the expensive upholstery.

As I have mentioned before, if you want more detailed instructions, there are a lot of books on this subject. Here, I will just cover the basic steps that I took. I used the old material as the pattern. By carefully dissecting it, you can figure out how it was originally done.

First, I needed six sheets of panel board for a four-door. (Panel board is a fiberboard that is ⅛ inch thick and normally sold in sheets of 30 × 40 inches. It is readily available at upholstery supply outlets.) The 30 × 40 panels were not quite big enough to cut two door panels per one sheet. Then I needed two sheets for the rear corners and back of the car. I had enough scrap to cover the small sections, like the kick panels.

My old door panel covers were in such bad shape that they weren't much use as a pattern for cutting new ones. I located the

This is my first attempt at sewing: tire covers for the spare tires.

window lift and door handles and punched out holes in the new panel, leaving plenty of room at the edge. I stapled the panel board to the doorframe with the top edge even with the window. I marked around the other three sides with a colored pencil. (The panel board is black.) I cut the straight lines with a utility knife and a straight-edge, about ⅛-inch inside the line. I wanted the panel to be a little smaller than the door, so that when I was covering the edges with the padding and fabric it wouldn't stick out past the edge of the door. If that happened the panel would rub on the doorpost or sill plate and wear out the fabric.

I marked each panel for its appropriate door and then on the upper backside so that I would always know which edge was the top, which side was the back, and which door it fit.

I tacked or stapled a ¾-inch strip of panel board around the upper interior of the car between the top bows on the sides and over the windshield and around the back, just at the point where the headliner would attach on the perimeter. Even if your car wasn't made this way, it is really helpful to have this guide strip.

I used a piece of corrugated cardboard with the corrugation vertical and pressed it into a rear corner of the car body. It needed to be long enough to reach from the rear doorpost to the center of the back. I kept it square with the doorpost and as near the top as it would go. At some point it would need to rest against the guidestrip that I had just installed. I then stapled the cardboard in place and trimmed it to the length at the center of the body. I used a compass like a divider and let the point follow along the guide strips. Keeping the point and pencil on a vertical plane, I followed the guide strip the length of the cardboard. I made sure that the compass was open enough to reach the farthest distance between the guide strip and the cardboard. I removed the cardboard and cut it along the line that I had just drawn.

I then checked the cardboard for fit and trimmed it where necessary. I pressed it into the opposite corner, bending it in the opposite direction. If it doesn't quite fit for you, adjust your guide strip to fit the cardboard. Both rear quarters of the body should be the same.

I measured the vertical distance where the panel board would cover at the rear doorpost and marked the panel board. I place the cardboard pattern I had just made on the mark and traced out the profile. I used the band saw on the curved cuts. It left the bottom of the cut rough but some sandpaper took the fuzz off with just a few passes. At this time, I left the panel board a little too long where it meets at the rear center of the car body. I then turned my pattern over and repeated the process for the opposite side.

After cutting both rear-quarter panel boards, I determined the distance from the rear doorpost to the start of the curve of the body. I marked this on the panel and placed the panel on a table and let it hang over the edge the distance from my mark-out. I put a board on the panel then added some weight on top of the board to hold it all down on the table. I made sure that one panel was turned opposite of the other. I c-clamped a one-by-four-inch board to the top and bottom of the panel board, just past the point where the curves would end. I left the panels hanging over the edge until I was ready for them. They would bend down slowly and set in time and be less apt to crease when pressed into the corner of the car body.

While the rear-quarter panels are forming to shape, I had a good opportunity to put in the headliner. When I restored my 1928 Dodge, I measured the length of the car body and the distance between the bows and then ordered a headliner with the bow strips or loops already sewn on. (On later vintage cars with steel bows that snap into place, you would need a loop to slide the bow through.) I had a difficult time tacking the headliner to the bows and at the same time keeping it straight and uniform. I had to start at the back of the car and tack or staple the first strip to the back bow and then move forward and repeat the process. Only after all of the strips were tacked in place could I tell how good a job I did. If I wanted to make more adjustments, I had to reverse the process back to where I needed to make the correction and start all over again. Maybe an expert seldom has any trouble, but I remember spending a long time with my Dodge headliner thinking that there must be a better way.

Remember to make sure that your fabric is wide enough. With the Franklin, I used fifty-four inches of fabric; the widest point of the headliner area was fifty-eight inches, so I sewed a four-inch strip on each edge toward the rear of the headliner. Be sure the nap, if there is any, runs in the same direction. If you have to do this with plaid or some type of print fabric, make sure that you also match the pattern allowing for the seam width. I had enough width to cover the headliner area, plus two inches of material for stapling on the sides. I cut the material to length, leaving enough trim to fasten front and rear. I marked a centerline on the backside of the headliner with tailor's chalk. I measured and marked the bow center-to-center distances on the back of the headliner, making sure that the lines were perpendicular to the center line and parallel to each other.

To install my headliner, I bought a roll of one-inch Velcro at the upholstery shop and stapled the hook side (the stiff nylon) half to the top bows and sewed the loop side to the headliner along the bowlines. I cut the Velcro about two inches shorter than the distance across the bow. (The Franklin is pretty square inside; if your car has more of a curve between the top bows and the sides, you may need to cut the Velcro even shorter.) I found the center (end-to-end) of the Velcro and aligned it with the centerline on the headliner and sewed it in place. I sewed one line of stitches down the center of the Velcro as straight as I could.

I discovered that if I rolled the headliner up from each end toward the bow line that I was working on, it was easier to handle and the bulk of material would pass through the sewing machine better.

I marked the center of each bow in the car and then aligned the centerline of the headliner, starting at the rear bow, then zipping the Velcro together. I moved to the next bow and did the same thing until I reached the front bow. If I had a wrinkle or too much slack between a couple of bows, I just unzipped the Velcro and adjusted it until it was uniform between the bows.

Starting at the center of one side of the car, I stapled the headliner on the perimeter by feeling the edge of the guide strip I had installed earlier for about one foot. Then I went to the opposite side and did the same. I worked from side to side toward the front and rear until I reach the corner. Then I worked across the front and rear from the center to the corner. By feeling the edge of the guide strip, it was easier to keep a uniform line and correct tension. Only after I was satisfied with the headliner, did I trim the excess material about an inch below the staple line.

By the time I completed the headliner, the rear quarter panels should have enough curve to be able to install them in the car without creasing them. I pressed them tightly into the corners of the car body and temporarily stapled them in place. I trimmed them to the exact length where they met at the center of the back of the car body. I cut out around the rear window even with the frame. I removed the panels and affixed the foam padding to them with spray-on adhesive. The gauze-reinforced type of padding tends to wrinkle in the corners when bent on an inside radius. I also kept the panels a little over-bent to what they will be when installed, while laminating the foam and fabric on them. This keeps the upholstery from wrinkling in the corners when they are installed.

I used a ¼-inch foam padding and trimmed it about ¼-inch from the edge of the panel. This gave me some padding on the edges without wrapping over the edge and creating too much bulk on the backside. Then I covered the panel with the upholstery fabric. I had to make sure that the nap lay downward on any vertical surface. I stretched the fabric vertically, pulled it over the edge and glued it into place with a hot glue gun. I made sure not to pull it tight horizontally or it would pull out of the corners.

On the Franklin, I didn't want the fasteners to show. I used spring clips along the bottom edge and center edge temporarily until

This photograph was taken after the upholstery was finished; you can see where the panel board is bent into the corner of the car body.

I got the upholstery to lie smooth and then glued along the top on the back. Before installing any panels, I put the windlace around the doorframes. Then I removed the spring clips from the quarter panel and installed it in the car by reaching under the fabric and tacking along the edge. Next I pulled it down tight and tacked through the upholstery along the bottom. The tacks won't show here when the seat cushion is put into place. I cut out around the rear window and stapled it. I tucked the upholstery under the panel along the rear centerline.

I tried to do the biggest section of the upholstery first so that any scrap piece can be used elsewhere, like on the door pockets (which I will cover next). Keep in mind that you will need a couple of long horizontal strips for the door header and vertical strips for the door post, especially if you are using a fabric with a pattern or a nap like the velour that I was using.

I mention this because if you cut the fabric too short, replacing it might be a challenge since the replacement fabric might come from a different dye lot that won't match very well. I should mention that when buying fabric, order a bit more than you think you need. That way if you make an error, you won't have to panic. I used ten yards of 54-inch fabric for the car interior and eight yards for the seats (which were a different color). I barely had enough for the interior, with only about four square feet left of the seat fabric.

The door panels were the next step. I took the old ones apart to study how they were originally made. The originals each had a pocket with a flap over the pocket. The flap had upholstery fabric on both sides, a stiffener in between and a steel bar along the bottom for weight.

I sewed the new flap using the fabric from an old flap for a pattern. I turned it right side out and slipped a piece of vinyl car top material inside of the flap for the stiffener and then top-stitched it on three sides. Two of the four steel bar weights were missing. The ones that I did have were rusty, so I made four new ones out of $\frac{1}{8}$-inch by $\frac{5}{8}$-inch galvanized bar that I picked up at the local hardware

store. I slid the weights to the bottom of the flap and sewed just above the bar to hold it in place like the original.

The pockets were simple enough, except that I couldn't find elastic as strong as the original rubber. I ended up using elastic twice as wide and doubling it over. The pouches were about twelve inches wide, but, because of the pleats, it took about eighteen inches of material.

The original door panels, each rectangular, had an insert piece of panel board around the pocket. This is where it is important to study the construction. (My Dodge has door pock-

Top: The right rear original door panel. It is in sad shape but taking it apart, I could study the construction details. *Bottom:* The pocket and flap from the dissected door panel.

128

ets also, but they were constructed completely differently.) I cut a hole in these inserts in the center with a two-inch border around where the pockets would be set.

As I mentioned, the door panels had been previously cut to size and marked for their respective doors. Using the panel as a guide, I cut the fabric and foam padding, leaving plenty of trim to fold over the edge of the panel. I located where the insert would be on the door panel. If you have a panel that is missing or deteriorated to a point that you can't tell where the pocket insert is supposed to be, like happened with the Franklin, assume the left front door measurements will be the same as the right front door.

Transfer the measurements of the location of the insert on the door panel to the upholstery fabric. Then place the insert on the

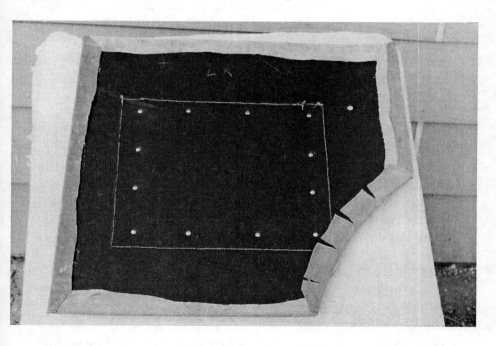

The back of the door panel, showing how I had to rivet the insert in place. Originally, it had been sewn in place.

back of the fabric and foam and cut the hole of the insert out, leaving enough material to fold over and glue to the insert.

I used the gauze-laminated foam on the doors. The reason for this is that non-fabric covered foam may be cut while sewing, causing a separation.

I placed the pocket and flap on the back of the insert and sewed it in place. Be sure to fold the door panel fabric back out of the way and just sew through the pocket or flap and the panel fabric that is glued to the insert. I cut a piece of fabric a little larger than the insert and glued it in place on the door panel so the fabric would be inside the door pocket.

I placed the assembly on the door panel where it was previously located. Originally these were sewn together, but my sewing machine didn't have the capacity to sew through two layers of panel board, plus the machine's arm didn't have enough reach to get to where I needed to sew. I went to "Plan B" and riveted the insert and panel board together with leather rivets.

I turned the door panel fabric right side up and pulled the fabric tight and held it in place with spring clips. The panel top was stretched around the edge of the insert so I used masking tape as a guide and sewed just inside of the tape. At this point you should put the panel fasteners in. (On my Dodge, which had all steel doors, I used spring-type fasteners that pushed through the holes in the door.) The Franklin originally used tack strips that nailed to the wood door framing. I didn't want to hammer on the fabric to drive the tack strip in place, so I used Velcro on the vertical edging screws along the top edge under the window frames. I put a strip of carpet along the bottom edge of the doors, holding it in place with screws and finish washers. These also held the door panel.

I turned the panel over and trimmed the foam down to about ¼-inch longer than the panel board. I glued the fabric in place as I removed the spring clips. I cut as small a slit as necessary in the fabric and foam for the window crankshaft and door latch shaft to pass through. Now the door panel was ready to install. I repeated this process for the rest of the doors. Actually, you will want to

The spring clips hold the fabric in place; the masking tape gives me a guide for the topstitching.

repeat each step for all of the doors as you proceed, thus saving time by not having to set up for each operation more than once.

The kick panels under the dash on each side can be covered with the floor carpet. The Franklin had a small pocket built in on the right side, so I made the pocket out of the upholstery fabric and covered the panels with the upholstery. Along the bottom edge, I carpeted on a line to match the carpet on the bottom of the door panels.

The door header and doorpost were upholstered next. I used some scrap ⅛-inch plywood for panel boards on the door header, because the panel board didn't come in a long enough length to reach all the way. I also cut all of the strips of panel board for the door window frames. I sprayed all of these small pieces with adhesive and stuck the pieces to the foam and then I cut the foam, leaving ¼-inch of it sticking out around each piece.

Here is the left front door panel, completed and installed.

I wrapped the fabric over the top of the door and windshield header strips and hot glued them in place. I installed the strips in the car by holding the fabric up out of the way and tacking the strips to the headers. (Don't tack too close to the bottom edge of the panel strips.) I tucked the upholstery fabric under the strip along the bottom edge. I couldn't buy a tucking tool at an upholstery shop, but it isn't really necessary. I just used a dull putty knife. I drove a few finish nails through the fabric along the bottom edge that also passed through the fabric on the other side. This would keep it in place. With a sharp pointed instrument, like a scribe, I pulled the fabric over the head of the nails. I fluffed the nap a little and the nail holes hardly showed.

On the door window frames, I used the same procedure, except I didn't need to tuck the fabric under. I worked from the outer edge to the window opening. I tacked the strips in place and brought the

The new armrest mount and the armrest are ready to install.

fabric into the inside of the window frame and stapled it down. The window frame molding covered the staples.

On the Franklin, the rear seat armrest and mounting wood needed to be replaced. It was simple enough just to saw new versions of both of these on the band saw. Originally, the mount was upholstered before the armrest was covered and screwed to the mount with wood screws. Then the fabric was tucked between the armrest and the rear quarter panel.

In my case, I thought that the fabric might work loose on the armrest, so I drilled through the armrest and the armrest mount. I put two carriage bolts through the armrest and covered it with padding and stapled the fabric in place. I upholstered the armrest mount, but left the bottom edge loose along where the rear seat cushion is placed. I put the armrest on the mount and reached up under the upholstery and installed the nuts on the carriage bolts and then tacked the upholstery in place. I installed the upholstered door-post panel strips. Now the car interior was completed and covered in fine fabric, except for the seat cushions.

I have described here in detail how I upholstered the Franklin, which has a wood-framed body. Wood framing was used quite extensively in this period, but not exclusively. My 1928 Dodge had an almost all-steel body, so some of the upholstery techniques were different.

The Dodge had metal tabs cut into the interior body metal that I could bend up and punch through the web on the windlace and then bend back down into place. Of course, some broke off, so I used sheet metal screws to hold the windlace in place where the tabs were broken.

The Dodge's headliner was installed the same way, except where I mentioned. I stapled it to the bows instead of using the Velcro trick. I fastened the edges of the Dodge headliner to a tack strip. The fiber tack strip had deteriorated, so I made a new one out of mahogany. I used mahogany because it holds a nail well and doesn't split easily. It is also rot resistant and I happened to have some scraps that would work.

Another difference with the Dodge was that the interior uphol-stery panels were installed with metal screws and finish washers instead of hidden fasteners. I needed to use the same holes where the screws were originally installed. To find the holes and align my new panels properly, I made a hole-finder out of a piece of ⅛-inch by ¾-inch steel bar about thirty inches long. I bent it into a sharp U so that the ends were even. I drilled a ⅛-inch hole in both ends so that the holes lined up. I put short metal screws through one hole from the inside so that the point sticks out.

Holding the panel against the car body, I slid the hole-finder over the panel edges and felt the point of the screw drop each time the hole-finder aligned with the hole in the car body. I would push an awl into the panel board to mark the location, remove the hole-finder, and install a sheet metal screw. I left the screws loose until all were located in each panel.

Every make of car will be different in technique and design of construction, but none is very difficult to figure out. Just remember, ordinary people put these cars together originally, so it doesn't take a genius to repeat the process.

With the interior upholstery now in the car, I installed the dome light and the switch on the doorpost.

The floorboards of the Franklin are flat except for the slope on the front floorboard. To make a pattern for the carpet and the carpet pad, I used newspaper and masking tape. By cutting and taping, I made a good fit around the pedals and levers.

I cut the felt carpet pad to fit up to about ½-inch from the sill plates. I also staggered the joints of the pad and carpet. I marked out the cut of the carpet on the backside. (Be sure to turn the pattern over.)

I sewed binding all around the carpet, except for the area that would go under the door sills. I left about ¾-inch to fit under the sill plates. After I made the front and back floor carpets, I cut the small pieces that fit around the seat base, front and rear. Even though the car wasn't originally made this way, I put four inches of carpet at the bottom of each door to protect the upholstery.

The backseat area had a carpeted footrest. I assumed that there must have been originally two of them so I made two new ones, using the old one as a pattern.

About all that was left to do was to upholster the seat cushions and the back. The Franklin cushion didn't have a back seat cushion. Someone had put a front cushion in the back as a replacement, but it was about six inches too short.

I used the hardware from the old, extra front seat cushion and made a frame to fit the rear cushion area. The old frame served as a pattern as far as design and construction detail. The spring set was approximately eight inches high at the front edge and four inches at the rear. I purchased enough coil spring to make four rows each of decreasing heights from eight to four inches. I made a border of edge wire and hog-ringed the assembly together. The spring set was then attached to the wood frame with staples over the lower-edge wire.

After removing the upholstery from the rest of the spring sets, I was ready to build up the cushions. If you have bare springs, it is a good idea to spray paint the spring-set with anti-rust paint. The original springs on the Franklin were burlap covered; removing the burlap and painting the springs was more work than I thought necessary, as their condition wasn't too bad. So, I just patched up the burlap and cleaned the springs out with compressed air.

I covered the springs with dense foam and reused the horsehair mat. Next,

I made the spring bed for the rear seat cushion with the store bought springs and edge wire.

I covered a layer of cotton batting with cotton duck cloth which I then hog-ringed to the spring set.

The seats were pleated in deep rolls. I had a professional do my Dodge seats (which were similar to the Franklin's), but the modern practice is to sew the upholstery fabric to a layer of foam, thus forming the pleats. That is the modern shortcut method, but the seats don't look or feel like the original rolled upholstery. So I decided to fashion my own for the Franklin.

I measured the width of the pleats on the under-fabric that, in this case, were four inches each. On the backside of the upholstery fabric, I marked out the distance over the pleats, which was five inches allowing for the seams. This can be determined by measuring whatever old seat covering you might have left.

I laid the upholstery fabric on top of the under-fabric. (I used cotton duck cloth underneath.) I folded the fabric back until the first line appeared right at the fold. I aligned this with the first line on the under-fabric and sewed as close to the fold as possible, keeping the line at the fold and the line on the under-fabric aligned and straight. I turned the seat cover around and folded the upholstery back to the line adjacent to the one I had just sewed. I rolled up the under-fabric close to the next line on it, so that it would fit through the sewing machine and then sewed the rest of the pleats in.

The under-fabric should lie flat and the upholstery fabric should have about one inch of slack between each pleat. The pleats on each end are not sewed to the under-fabric on the edge of the seat.

To stuff the cotton batting in the pleats I determined how much cotton would fill the pleat. I had one inch batting and cut an eleven-inch strip off the end of the roll and folded them over so that they were about two inches thick and 5½-inches wide. (These are approximate measurements as it is hard to measure cotton batting with any degree of accuracy.)

I made a plastic sleeve about twice as long as the distance through the pleat. I slid the cotton into the sleeve and passed the empty end of the sleeve through the pleat. I held the seat cover and pulled the sleeve and cotton into the pleat until it was almost through. I made a push stick about one-by-three-inches wide and about two feet in length. I knocked off the sharp edges so that it wouldn't tear the plastic sleeve. I slid the push stick in place by resting it against my belly and holding the seat cover with one hand and pulled the sleeve out with the other. (You might ask a friend or wife to help, if you still have either by this stage of the restoration.) I ended up with a nice, even pleat; it was a lot quicker than trying to stuff the cotton batting in.

After filling all of the intermediate pleats, I pulled out any excess cotton on each end. I sewed a strip of vinyl onto the back edge of the cushion and the bottom of the backrest. This saved some upholstery fabric, but it also makes it easier to slide the seat cushion in place. I centered the covering on the spring assembly and tacked it into place on the wood frame. If you are attaching it to a metal frame, you will have to hog-ring it on.

I worked from the center of the front of each cushion and then repeated the process on the back, leaving the ends open. I next stuffed the cotton batting into the end pleats. I put a little extra at the front corner of the cushion and pulled it down into place and tacked it to the seat frame. I repeated the process for the other cushions and backs.

This shows the technique that I used to stuff the pleats into the seat cushions.

This is the front seat back: notice the half-round trim molding around the edge.

The backrest on the Franklin was a metal frame with tack-strips nailed to the metal to attach the upholstery. The tack-strips were curved to fit the frame which would fit the contour of the car body. I made new tack-strips by laminating three layers of ⅛-inch plywood strips and fastening them to the metal frame with pop rivets.

Before I covered the backrest on the front seat of the Franklin I had to upholster the wings, i.e. the outer edges of the back rest.

I masked off all of the upholstery on the seat back, then sprayed adhesive to the backside of the front seat wing and attached to that area a layer of ¼-inch foam padding. I trimmed the padding along the edge and covered the backside of the front seat wing with upholstery fabric and then tacked it into place along the edge over the top of the backrest covering.

139

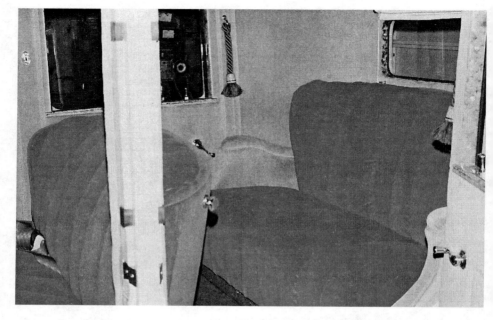

The finished product of my first complete upholstery project.

The Franklin had a trim strip to cover the tacks on the seat edge made out of half-round reed. I covered this trim with foam padding and upholstery and glued it to the underside. I then nailed it into place with finish nails driven through the fabric. After pulling the fabric over the nail heads and fluffing up the nap, the nail holes hardly showed at all.

Some cars use a hide-'em welt to cover the upholstery tacks. This welt opens in the center so that you can tack it in place, then closes up and hides the tack heads. I installed the seat back in the car, discovering in the process that it is easier to put the front seat in first through the back door and then move the seat forward.

The backrest of the back seat hung on a couple of brackets and was held in place with a wood screw at the bottom corners.

I couldn't find a suitable cord to make a robe cord, so I used what I could find and covered it with the seat upholstery fabric. I made the rear window blind out of a piece of silk that was very similar to the original. The pull straps for the rear seat were made out of drapery cord of comparable size to the original. I installed the ashtray on the back of the front seat and shut the door.

The interior of the car was finished.

CHAPTER 11

The Test Drive

There were a couple more details before the car would be ready for a test drive.

I needed tire-mount mirrors for the Franklin that are available, but would cost $400 about a pair and wouldn't be authentic anyway. So, I decided to make some. I sawed the base out of ¼-inch aluminum plate on the band saw. I then made a wood form to bend them to fit the contour of the spare tires. The tires were of a 32-inch diameter or a 16-inch radius. Due to the spring back of the metal, I ended up with a 13-inch radius on my form. I cut the arch in a piece of scrap oak and put the aluminum between the two halves of the form and drew them together with bar clamps. This gave me an even arch the length of the base. Since I was custom-making the mirror mounts, I designed them long enough to line up with the straps that would hold the spare tire in place. I turned the mirror post out of a 1½-inch aluminum round stock and drilled and tapped two ¼-inch holes to attach them to the base. Then I drilled and tapped a hole on the upper end to attach the mirror. I angled the post out 30 degrees to give better visibility.

On the fender at the center of the wheel well was an anchor bolt for the spare tire lock. I wasn't too concerned about locking the tire in place, but I didn't like the look of the anchor on the fender.

I made a wood model of what I determined the lock to be like and sent it to be cast in stainless steel. After receiving the locks back, I mounted them and the car was ready for a test run.

I drove the car about five miles and returned to my shop. Right

Forming the tire mirror base. I used more clamps than shown here, but for clarity I am just showing two of them.

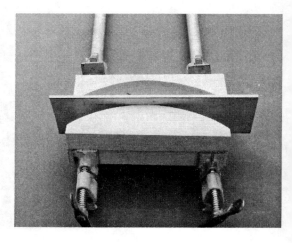

away I could tell that the steering was a bit too loose, so I adjusted the slack out of the steering gear box. I had an oil leak in the over-drive that was a simple fix.

One thing that will need attention after a hundred miles or so

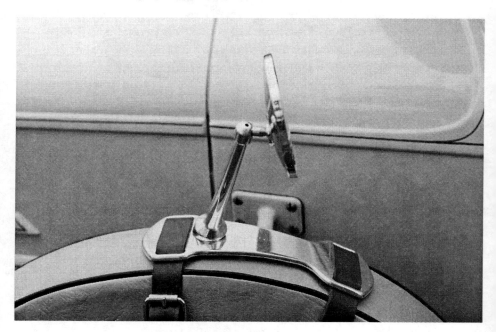

The finished mirror. I buffed the aluminum to give it a shiny finish like the chrome.

will be the brakes. After the lining wears some, I will need to adjust them in order to get the correct contour to fit the drums. Further adjustments will occur at a lot longer intervals. I also would check the spring U bolts after the springs have worked in. I used a torque wrench on these, as it would be difficult to feel the torque that I would apply when compressing the spring

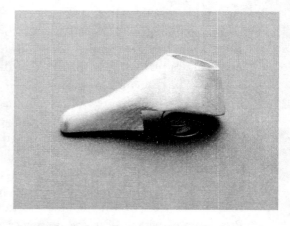

A wood model of my spare tire lock. I sent it off to be cast in stainless steel.

leaves. For safety, I will check the critical joints such as the spring shackles, tie rod ends, drag link and kingpins.

I checked the valve lash to make sure that I had adequate clearance after the valves had a chance to seat in. If you don't have a manual for your engine, set the valves .006-inch to .007-inch minimum clearance. Overhead valves should be set with the engine hot.

After you have completed the restoration of your car, you will need to drive it quite a lot to make sure that everything will function properly in the long run. If you are going to do the Great American Race, as I did with my 1928 Dodge, it is really important to get all of the bugs worked out. A major breakdown during the cross-country rally would ruin the experience for you, not to mention the cost involved. Also, breakdowns sometimes happen at the most inopportune times and places.

It is even more important to have the car thoroughly tested when you are trying to keep the cost down during the restoration. This was the case with the Franklin. I used the old pistons, which were good enough, but I needed new rings. The bore on the Franklin is 3½-inch standard and this engine was bored .060" oversize. This made the bore of the cylinders close to 3⁹⁄₁₆". I checked my

parts book and found the 235 cubic inch Chevrolet engine is 3⁹⁄₁₆"
and the parts are readily available, so I bought a set of Chevy piston
rings. Only then to find they were too thin for the ring grooves for
my Franklin pistons, plus the fact that the Franklin had four ring
pistons. The Chevrolet rings would fit if I used the oil scraper rings
as spacers on the compression rings. This meant that I had to get
two sets of rings to have enough for the oil rings and spacers.

After doing this, everything worked fine. The engine ran well,
until it got warmed up. I had checked the ring end gap so that I
would know if it was okay. But then, as the engine got hot, it
worked harder, which made more heat. It was one of those progres-
sive things: More heat made more work, which makes more heat.
Pretty soon I had all heat and no power and the hood was too hot to
touch.

I will probably never know what the problem was for sure, but
my guess is that there was too much piston-ring friction and too
much oil scraped off of the cylinder walls. Plus, with over 100-degree
days here in Arizona and it being an air-cooled engine, it just wasn't
going to work. So back to the shop and the proverbial old drawing
board. Here is where I tried to save a buck, but outsmarted myself: I
ended up buying new pistons and rings anyway.

One good thing about the air-cooled Franklin was that I could
just unbolt the cylinders from the crankcase and pull them off of the
pistons. In fact, I didn't even have to get under the car. I left the
whole bottom end intact. The piston pins are held in with a pinch
bolt at the small end of the connecting rod. After all the cylinders
were off, I turned the engine until the two pistons would be at the
top-dead center. I would have enough room to get at the pinch bolt.
After I removed it, I just slid the piston pins out and had the entire
piston off the rods. After removing the heads from the cylinders, I
was ready to start over, as far as the engine work was concerned.

I had never rebuilt an air-cooled automobile engine before and
I already messed up once, so I was determined to get it right this
time. I had some experience with air-cooled diesel engines while I
was working on the Alaska Pipeline, but that was a cost-plus project

and we just replaced everything. As I said earlier, a good mechanic should be able to make an intelligent decision on what to save and what to replace. Of course, the key word here is intelligent and I obviously ran out of talent momentarily.

I thought that I would save $40 on the piston rings that I now couldn't use. So, to make up for that, I bought new pistons with low-friction rings for $300 and a $300 rigid hone. By using a rigid hone, I could get the cylinders closer to being round and could feel any taper in them. I honed the cylinders until I got a slight drag pushing the piston through with a strip of .005-inch shim along the major thrust side of the piston.

After replacing the cylinder heads, I was ready to put them back together. I used a clamp-type ring compressor with the bottom-side up. This way I could push the cylinder down onto the piston; then by taking the ring compression apart, I could get it off from around the connecting rod.

Everything went back together, as it should have, with no problems. After a test run I was sure I had the heating problem fixed. I decided on a further improvement by installing an oil cooler, mounting it above the blower housing in back of the shutters where the ram air would blow through it. I had installed a 235-Chevrolet oil pump so there was plenty of oil in circulation. The oil went from the pump through the full-flow oil filter and then through the cooler and back to the engine bearing.

With these changes, I had a really cool-running Franklin engine. This was confirmed after a few more test drives. But I discovered I was still having excess oil on and around the cylinder heads.

Franklin engines of this era oil the rocker arms and valves with a pump mounted on the firewall. As a weight in the pump bounces up and down, it sends a shot of oil onto the felt pads above the rocker arms. The oil that gets into the rocker box has no way to return, so some seepage is normal. I emptied the oil reservoir on the firewall pump, but I was still getting oil on the cylinder heads. Where was it coming from was the big question.

Sometimes a rotating part will sling the oil off so completely that it never feels oily to the touch. If you suspect that this might be the case, a good test is to hold a piece of cardboard in line with the plane of the flywheel, pulley, etc. If oil is leaking around the shaft and being thrown off, it will leave a streak of oil on the cardboard. In order to do this test on the Franklin, I removed the timing hole cover on the right side of the blower housing. Then I cut a piece of cardboard that would fit through the hole and be long enough to reach the back of the blower. With the engine running, I held the cardboard in place for about 20 seconds. Sure enough, there was a streak of oil on it.

My conclusion was that with the higher volume of oil I was getting with the Chevy oil pump and the fact I was using 10–40 oil, the oil slinger on the crankshaft wouldn't handle it. I suspected there was also a bit of negative pressure near the hub of the blower. The oil was being thrown off the backside of the blower, then picked up in the cooling air stream and deposited on the cylinder heads.

I took the front of the engine apart again and removed the timing chain cover. I measured the outside diameter of the blower hub where a seal would ride if it had one. After checking my seal catalog, I found a seal to fit the hub. I then had the timing chain cover bored out to fit the bore size of the seal. With everything back in place, I was ready for another test drive.

After two or three hundred miles of driving the car, I was really pleased with how well it ran. The more you drive your car with no problems, the more your confidence increases. I installed an aftermarket tachometer to give me an idea of how fast the engine was turning at different road speeds. (A tachometer isn't allowed in the Road Rally rules, but if I did another Rally I could remove it.) I discovered that I really didn't need the overdrive that I installed. The car would go 60 mph in direct at 2500 RPM and 60 mph at 2000 RPM in overdrive. Sixty was fast enough for me in this old car and 2500 RPM wasn't turning the engine too fast. The cooling air for the engine is in direct proportion to the engine speed.

It takes the same amount of energy to propel the car 60 mph

whether in overdrive or not, which relates to the heat the engine produces. I concluded that I was reducing the cooling air by 20 percent in overdrive, but producing the same heat. Plus the engine speed seemed to lug down with the slightest incline.

I removed the overdrive and the cross member that I had installed earlier. I mentioned before that I was going to have a new driveline made up, but I never got around to doing it. This car used early Spicer universal joints. They have a cross like a modern U joint, but use hardened steel bushings instead of cups with needle bearings. The U joint is covered with a spherical shield that holds the grease with an outer shield that oscillates over the inner one. Thus, the U joint is completely enclosed. I cleaned the driveline and the U joints and then repacked the grease shield with grease and painted the whole thing. I bolted it back in place between the drive flanges as originally installed.

Well, I was back on the road again and happy as a clam at high tide for about 100 miles. Then the car developed a vibration in direct proportion to the road speed. It was the familiar bad U-joint type of vibration. I nursed the car home at a slow speed and sure enough one of the bushings had worked out of place.

The bushings are held in place with a perimeter wire that fits in a groove on the outside of the bushing and a matching groove in the bore of the yoke. The bushing had worked loose and rotated enough in the bore to work the wire out of place.

The idea came to me that maybe I could find a modern U joint to fit the yokes. The groove in the bore of the yokes was too small and too near the inner edge of the bore to use a snap ring as a modern U joint uses. The inside of the yoke was cut square with the bore, so I figured a U joint with the C clip toward the center of the cross would work. The bore in the yoke was $1\frac{1}{16}$-inch, so I went to the auto parts store and looked through their U joint book. I had the measurement across the inside of the yokes, so I looked for a C clip U joint with $1\frac{1}{16}$-inch cups.

They had two sizes to choose from in the distance from the outside of the C clip across the cross. One size was too big and one

UNIVERSAL JOINTS

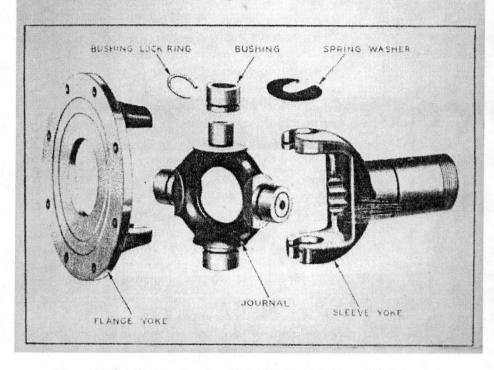

BUSHING LOCK RING   BUSHING   SPRING WASHER

JOURNAL

FLANGE YOKE   SLEEVE YOKE

Diagram of the original universal joint which shows all of the details. I replaced the original cross and bushings with a modern cross and cups. From the Franklin owner's manual, 1930.

was too small. I bought two of the too-small sizes. They measured .100-inch too short to fit the yokes on the driveline. So I made eight 1¹⁄₁₆-inch washers that were .050-inch thick. By putting these over the cups between the inside of the yokes and the C clips, I had a modern U joint installed. I put the grease shield back in place and from the outside, no one could tell of the improvement that I had made. I never made any changes to the original parts, so the original U joints could be installed if I wanted to.

Okay, I was back on the road again. I felt I had worked the

bugs out of the car after the completed restoration. A few hundred miles later it was still performing excellently. I was ready for a long trip of which I will tell later.

I took in numerous car shows, driving the car to all of them. Also, when my wife and I wanted to take a pleasure drive for a day or go to visit friends in another town, we would drive the Franklin instead of our regular car. The people seemed surprised that I drove my car that much. They would ask how I kept it running so well. I didn't want to tell them about all of the trouble I had just after it was restored, but I offered some tips on maintaining an old car. After all, cars were made to drive and that is what I had intended for this one in the first place.

CHAPTER 12

Maintaining Your Car

I have been asked about maintaining a car after it has been restored or at least fixed up well enough to drive. I will try to answer the most frequent concerns that I get from people. This is what has worked for me, but I am not implying that this is the last word in maintenance.

First, I will discuss the engine oil. If you have an old car that you just want to get running again, I would recommend pulling the oil pan and cleaning the sludge out of it. Also, clean the oil pump screen and the rest of the engine as best as you can. Cars before the mid–1950s usually had a bypass oil filter. Be sure to replace it if you can find a new one. A lot of times the filters have been removed. Even an old bypass filter is better than none. There are adapters that you can get at the bigger auto parts stores and you can adapt a modern spin-on-filter to your engine. Some clubs — depending on the make of car — have adapters for modern filters that are installed inside the original canister. This gives you a modern filter with the original look on the outside.

Most cars up to the late 1920s used a splash-type oil system. Chevrolet used this system up into the 1950s. The system had an oil pump that would pump oil into a galley or trough. It drained down into the main bearings. The excess oil filled troughs in a windage plate in the oil pan where the dippers on the connecting rod scooped it up. This type of engine only had four or five pounds of oil pressure. If your engine hasn't been thoroughly cleaned, then use non-detergent oil. Detergent oil will loosen all of the gunk and plug up the oil passages, but if the engine has been thoroughly cleaned, like when it has been rebuilt, then use detergent oil to keep it clean. For a splash-oil system, use a straight 30-weight oil.

For pressure oil system engines, use the lightest oil that will maintain 25 pounds of pressure or more. If you can't maintain 25 pounds of oil pressure with 30-weight oil, you need to take up the bearings. Again, if the engine hasn't been cleaned, use non-detergent oil. After the engine has been thoroughly cleaned, using a detergent oil is the best. I also use a 10–40 weight oil after I rebuild an engine. You can install a full-flow oil filter if you are not concerned with exactly duplicating the original condition of the car.

Regarding the transmission oil, some old cars call for 600-weight steam oil in the transmission because that was the only kind they had back then. I have read where there are still some sources for purchasing it, but it is not readily available. The gears in these old cars were cut with plenty of clearance. The heavy oil made them run quieter. After the 1930s transmissions used synchronizers which were made of brass or bronze. Some people are concerned about using this heavy "hypoid" gear oil since it does contain sulfur.

Sulfur, under the right conditions of moisture, will form sulfuric acid (H_2SO_4). As you can see from the chemical symbols it is made up of sulfur and water. The acid etches away the brass or bronze. The old timers used to put baking soda in the transmission to neutralize that problem. I wouldn't do this, because the abrasive qualities of the soda would do more harm than a little acid.

Modern gear oil, like engine oil, has polymers in it and is multigrade like 90–140 weight. The thinking now is that the lighter the oil the better. I have had no problems using modern gear oil in any of my old cars. If the transmission is a bit noisy due to torsional vibrations, just add a pint of STP oil treatment. This makes the oil stick to the gears and quiets it down considerably. As far as any acid forming in the gearbox, it shouldn't be a problem if you drive your car periodically. But for a car that sits a long time in humid conditions, then changing the gear oil couldn't hurt. The differential, or rear end, gear oil that I use is the same as the transmission's. Some people are concerned that the lighter and more modern gear oil won't lubricate well enough.

The early cars used straight-cut bevel gears in the rear end. Later, spiral-bevel gears came out which were much quieter. These were both just straight mesh, due to the fact that the centerline of the pinion and ring gears are on the same plane.

When Packard came out with the hypoid gears, it created more of a lubrication problem. They lowered the pinion shaft and gear below the plane of the ring gear centerline. This caused a wiping or rubbing action as the gear meshed, which is why hypoid gear oil was developed, the point being that the hypoid gear oil should be more than adequate for straight- or spiral-bevel gears.

Now to the chassis lube. If you have a show car and want it to have the original look, keep the original grease fittings. I have a coffee can full of the old cross-pin type, cone-shaped and even grease cup fittings. They all worked in their day, but for a car that is driven regularly, I use the modern nipple grease fittings. The grease fittings help get the grease into the joints that need lubrication. I feel the modern ones do the job best. If I want the car to have the original look, then it is not much effort to change them.

Some car owners that I have talked with are concerned about lithium-based grease. They claim that it turns hard and causes wear in the joints. It might, but I have never seen it. If it doesn't happen here in an Arizona climate, I don't know where it would and if it did, it would take a long time to cause any problems.

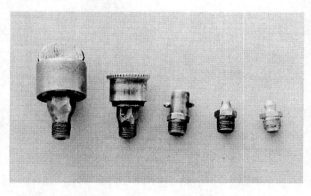

From left to right are two styles of grease cups, a cross pin grease fitting, a cone-style of grease fitting and a modern grease fitting. They are all ⅛-inch pipe thread.

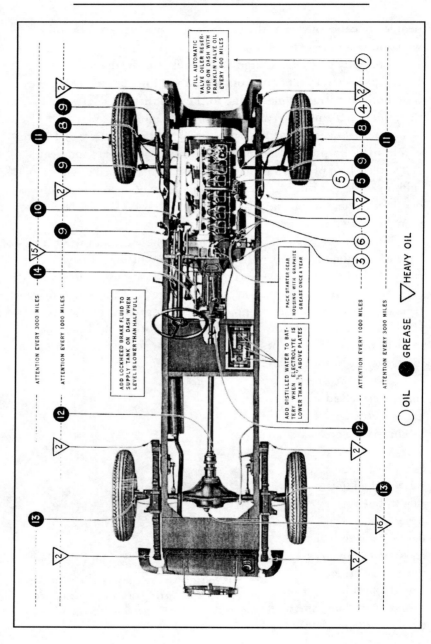

I grease the chassis a couple times a year and wipe off the excess so that I always have fresh grease in the joints. Under the conditions which an old car is used, any chassis grease should be fine.

There are a few more maintenance items that you will have to deal with that don't apply to modern vehicles.

All of the old cars that I have seen use string packing and nut to seal the water pump shaft. I mentioned this in Chapter 5, explaining the modification that I have made using a modern pump seal. This may not be practical or desirable, so if you stay with the original seal, you will need to adjust the nut to tighten the seal periodically. If the car has been sitting a long time, or if there is no room for adjustment left, you will have to replace the seal packing.

To replace the seal packing, remove the water pump from the engine and take the pump apart. With the shaft out of the pump body and the nut removed, use a hook (an O ring hook works good) to pull all of the old packing out. Be sure you get it all. The shaft will probably be worn down in the area where the packing seals are on it. If the diameter of the shaft is worn ¹⁄₁₆-inch or less in diameter than the original shaft, it should be usable if it doesn't have any rust pits. Polish the shaft with some emery cloth to remove any sharp ridges or surface rust. Also, check the shaft for straightness.

If you find that the pump shaft isn't usable, I would recommend replacing it with stainless steel. They are available for common cars like a Model A Ford, or you can have one made at a machine shop. You can use ⅛-inch string packing, which is available at major hardware stores or plumbing supply outlets. I like the old, impregnated string better than the Teflon string packing.

Push the end of the packing string into the bore around the shaft. Go around the shaft in a clockwise direction, pushing it to the bottom of the bore with a thin screwdriver. Continue pushing the

Opposite: **This lubrication chart shows all of the points to contend with in the 1930 Franklin. I copied this from the 1930 Franklin owner's manual.**

157

packing in until there is about ¼-inch of thread left showing in the bore. Screw the nut back in until it is snug and you can turn the shaft by hand with some effort. If the nut goes in more than halfway, add more packing. Some pumps have an external nut (female thread) that screws onto the pump body, but the procedure is still basically the same.

After you have installed the pump back on the engine and filled it with water, check for leaks. If some water leaks out, tighten the nut just enough to stop the leak. But don't overtighten it. Sometimes a pump will draw air in around the packing with the engine running and not leak water when it is stopped. If you suspect this may be a problem, a good test is to run your car down a long hill with the engine up to speed, but using very little throttle so you are not producing much heat. If the water surges out then there is a good chance air is getting into the cooling system. Try tightening the packing nut a little more. If this doesn't stop the problem, you may have to either replace the pump shaft or check for another source that is letting air get into the system.

You can rev the engine up and watch the lower radiator hose. If it collapses and shuts off the water flow, this will create a vacuum in the system, causing air to get in. This will also create a heating problem at higher engine speeds. Replacing the hose or putting a wire spring inside of it can cure this.

The generator is probably the component that is the most prone to problems. This is why the alternator was one of the first electronic devices installed on cars. I will try to explain how a generator works as an approach to troubleshooting the charging system.

A generator produces electricity by passing a winding through a magnetic field. On early generators, the field was of the permanent magnet type, like a magneto (which is a high-voltage generator). The windings are the armature: the more winding and the faster they pass through the magneto field, the more current and voltage is produced. As a winding passes through the field, it produces a current after it turns 180 degrees; then it produces a current again but in the opposite direction. The term alternator was derived from the fact that it produces an alternating current. The older generators did too, but to get a direct current they used a commutator: the brushes picked off the current in one direction only. They just used a mechanical switch whereas the alternator uses diodes to control the current direction.

The permanent magnet generators didn't stay in use long, since there was no way to control the output. The next step in development was the electromagnetic field. By controlling the field current, you could control the generator output. An adjustable third brush could pick off some of the current and voltage to excite the field. This brush is out of phase, so the voltage in the field circuit is about half of the output voltage. By moving the third brush closer to the main brush, the field voltage will increase, which of course will increase the output voltage and current. Move the third brush away from the main brush and it will decrease the voltage and current. As the speed of the armature increases with the engine speed, the output also increases. As the armature turns, it tends to drag the magnetic field with it, pulling it away from the third brush. This has the effect of decreasing the current picked off for the field circuit. This phenomenon makes this system self-regulating to some degree.

The next step in development was the voltage regulator. The voltage and current (amperes) are parallel: increasing one will increase the other. I know this is not completely true, but for the mechanic troubleshooting a system, it is close enough.

The voltage regulator uses electromagnetic switches and resistors to control the voltage. The field circuit comes from the generator through a resistor, then through the field windings. As the generator picks up speed, the magnetic switch pulls the contact points from the high output resistor circuit to a lower output circuit by routing it through more resistance, which will decrease the field voltage. Regulators got more complicated with more switches as advancements were made, including a vibrator to help control the current.

The generator also must have a cutout so that the battery voltage won't feed back through the generator when the engine isn't running or running too slow to make the generator function. In the early three-brush generators, the cutout was usually mounted on the generator. When voltage regulators came into use, the cutout was usually mounted inside the regulator box.

I am sure you have heard the story that you can push a car to start it with a completely dead battery if it is equipped with a generator. This is true if the generator has some residual magnetism left in it. The natural magnetism in the field will start the process. Then the field gets excited which causes the generator to put out enough current to make the ignition system work and the engine start. If the generator has lost all of its residual magnetism, then the process won't work. Sometimes if a generator hasn't been used in a long time, you may have to excite the field by using a jumper wire from a hot wire to the field wire. This only takes a momentary contact, which will restore the magnetism in the field. If your generator quits working, you will need to troubleshoot the problem. Always start with the simple things first.

To check your generator, first check the amp meter — if the battery isn't dead it, should show discharge when you turn the lights on, with the engine not running. If the bridge is burned out in the amp meter, the lights won't work and the generator won't charge the battery. Put a jumper wire across the terminals on the back of the meter. Make sure it is at least 12-gauge wire for a six-volt system. If the lights work, you have probably found the problem. Start the engine and watch the headlights; speed up the engine. If the lights get brighter, then you know the generator is working, even thought the amp meter isn't.

This will work until you can replace the amp meter. Most of these old cars only had a 20- or 30-amp meter. When I put a single-wire alternator on in place of the generator, they are usually 60-amp alternators. To avoid burning out the amp meter, I put a jumper wire across the terminals on the meter. It won't read true amperage, but it will show charge or discharge, which is what you are most concerned with anyway.

If your amp meter is working, then check the generator.

Remove the band or cover over the brushes. If your generator is belt-driven, make sure the belt is tight enough. Start the engine and speed it up to a high idle. There should be some sparks coming from the brushes where they contact the commutator. If there are no sparks, try cleaning the commutator with an eraser. Use the gray ones that are made to erase ink; they contain some abrasive. If this doesn't help, shut off the engine and check if the brushes are making good contact and also look to see if there are any beads of solder in the brush area of the generator. With no solder present and the brushes making good contact on the commutator, check the field circuit. On some of these three-brush generators, like the Northeast, there is a fuse for the field under a plug on the brush end of the generator. Others may have a fuse mounted on the generator cutout. Regulated generators may have a fuse on the regulator. In any case, check the fuse for the field circuit. If the fuse is okay, next check the generator cutout. If you have a belt-driven generator, remove the belt. Press the contacts on the cutout together and if the generator spins like a motor, it is probably okay. You can also try cleaning and adjusting the cutout contacts. The cutout should close at around 800 RPM. If it doesn't, bend the tab stop or adjust the spring tension so that the contacts close at the right speed. Make sure they open when you stop the engine.

On a chain-driven generator, you will have to remove it to do the motor test. Be sure to just remove the generator and not the adjuster plate because it holds the chain-idle sprocket — if you are not careful, you may get the engine out of time or loosen the sprocket inside the chain housing.

If the generator runs like a motor, then your problem must be in the regulator. This can be confirmed by manually operating the regulator contacts. This test has to be done before removing the drive belt and with the engine running at a fast idle. I have never seen a chain-driven generator that used a regulator; they were all three-brush types, as far as I know.

Regulators can be adjusted, but you will need some electrical test equipment and the specs for the particular regulator that you are testing. Check it over and clean the contacts and also look to make sure none of the resistors are burned out. It has been my experience that once a regulator quits working correctly, it is difficult to adjust it to work with any consistency.

If your generator still doesn't want to run after the motor test, try turning it by hand to get it started. If it turns on its own, then stop after part of a rotation, it probably means that an armature segment has either an open or a short circuit. The armature overheating and breaking down the insulation on the windings would most likely cause a short circuit. If the windings are black and have a burned smell, you will need to have the armature rewound or replaced. An open circuit can be caused by overheating too, as it melts the solder where the windings fasten to the commutator. Resolder any loose wires and test for a short circuit. Any continuity between the commutator and the steel plates of the armature will indicate that.

Brushes that do not make good contact may also cause an open circuit. After you have cleaned the commutator with the eraser, it should be easy to see if you have any grooves or flat spots. In this case, put the armature in the lathe and turn down the commutator just enough to true it up. Be sure to undercut the insulation between the segments. I use an old hacksaw blade by grinding the sides down to make it thinner and to remove any set in the teeth. Cut just below the segments; you don't need to overdo it.

If you can't get the right replacement brushes for your generator, get some that are a little too big and file them down to fit. Be sure to file the contact end to match the contour of the commutator. Don't use starter brushes as they are too hard for the generator with the constant use it gets.

Check to see if the armature has been dragging on the field sections. There are only three reasons that would happen: a bad bearing, a bent armature shaft or a loose field section. Simple tests for any of these factors should isolate any problems in the charging system. It takes no special equipment and can be done quicker than you can write them down.

If your generator overheats, as indicated by the color of the windings and the smell, you will need to find out why this is happening. The most likely reason is that the generator is putting out too much current. The field voltage controls the output, so the regulator isn't working right or the third brush needs adjusted for less output. The battery may have a bad cell so the voltage never gets high enough for the regulator to know when it is charged up enough. This shouldn't cause the generator to overheat, but it will work a lot harder than it should.

The ignition systems need attention quite often, especially the breaker points. When your collector car sits without running for a long time, the points corrode and won't make contact when you finally try to start it up. This is easy to fix by cleaning the points up with a point file. They should be readjusted for the proper gap. If you don't know the specs of your car, set the points at .019-inch–.020-inch for a four- or six-cylinder car and .015-inch–.016-inch for an eight-cylinder car.

With the distributor cap off and the switch on, pull the coil wire out of the cap and hold it about a half-inch from the engine. Open and let the points close several times with a screwdriver. You should get a blue spark with a snapping sound. If you are not getting a spark, try moving the coil wire closer to the ground source. When the wire is about ⅛-inch from the engine and you get a weak spark or none at all, the condenser could be bad. Disconnect the original condenser and install a new one. There is a lot of controversy as to what capacity of condenser to use. Unless you have a way of knowing what your car is supposed to have and the means to test the condenser, it is a moot point. Get one for a six-volt system, if that is what your car has and it will work fine. I usually ask for points and a condenser for old six-volt Chevrolets, which seem to be available most of the time. With a new condenser and good spark, you have solved the problem. Some condensers made for the old cars were of a special shape and design, so if you want to preserve the original look, conceal the new condenser as close to the points as you can.

The coil is the next thing to check. In a lot of the old cars, the ignition switch was built into the base of the coil and mounted under the dash. Over the years the coil would swell up, breaking the insulation around the switch. These old switches are hard to find in good condition. If an original style switch and coil can't be found, then the only option is to mount a universal switch and a modern coil. This is what I did with the Franklin and unless you looked under the dash, you couldn't tell the difference.

With a new coil and a good spark, you may want to try your original condenser again. For myself, I would stay with the new condenser, but then I am not into cars for show.

Breaker points may be hard to find for some old cars or too expensive if you find some new-old-stock originals. I have used Delco points in a lot of distributors by modifying the base of the points. Drill new mounting holes, or if close, elongate them to fit the distributor plate. I have modified quite a few old pre-window Delco distributors to fit different engines. This takes some machine work, so if you don't have a lathe, it wouldn't be practical to have it done because of the time involved. But if you can modify a distributor, this allows you to use readily available points that last longer than the original, plus you can save the original distributor for show. This is important with some cars, where the pot metal distributors tend to disintegrate, like my Dodge with the Northeast distributor.

An old style Delco distributor with an electronic pick-up in place of the points. This was not allowed in the "Great American Race" rally.

One problem I have encountered with old distributors concerns the vacuum advance that rotates the distributor plate. The engine may run fine, but then cut out. Everything looks normal, but there is a ground wire under the distributor plate a few inches long. It grounds the plate to the body of the distributor and after years of bending, it breaks off. The engine may run fine until the plate moves, then it doesn't ground, and with the ground wire broke, it is like turning off the engine. After the engine stops, the vacuum is lost, the distributor plate moves and makes a ground connection again. This makes for difficult troubleshooting.

Another thought on distributors is finding the correct distributor cap and rotor. Some are quite hard to find, if not impossible. Your next best choice is to find one that will fit or be close to it with some modifications. The rotor needs to match the cap for height, diameter and direction. It is best to remove the distributor from the engine while trying to fit up the cap and rotor. If it locks up while turning it by hand, nothing is hurt but some damage is bound to occur in the engine.

Try different caps until you find one that is the right diameter. The locking clip can be relocated if necessary to match the cap. The tang or keyway that holds the cap from rotating can be moved also, or file a new notch in the cap. Once you have a cap, then match the rotor to it. If your rotor is too long, file the end off a bit. When it is too low, you can cut some shims out of gasket paper and put it between the distributor shaft and the rotor. The rotor needs to be pointing to a post on the cap when the points open. If it is not, you can change the rotor by removing the key, or flat areas, with a die grinder, then drill and tap the side of the rotor to make room for a small setscrew. Once you have the setscrew in the right location and depth, lock it in place with some epoxy glue. Your other option is to move the points to match the rotor. Drill and tap the distributor plate to remount the points a few degrees so they open when the rotor is pointing to a post.

This gives you three options to get the cap, rotor and points synchronized. Modify the one that takes the least effort and try to keep as close to the original parts as possible.

The cotton-braided, yellow and black spark-plug wires are a source of trouble with cars that still have them. They work when they are new, but with heat and time, the lacquer coating breaks down. The insulation draws moisture, which causes the voltage to leak out, leading to a misfire in the engine.

If you are restoring a car using this wire to get the original look, it is really best to make up a set of spark-plug wires for show. Generally, it takes very little effort to remove the distributor cap wire and shroud as a unit for switching around. This way you can keep the spark-plug wires looking new just for the shows. But for driving, if you have an extra distributor cap, make up a set with a modern spark-plug wire. It is best not to use the metal shroud anyway. Get some snap-on wire separators at your auto parts store to keep the wires in order. The engineers of the time didn't understand the effects of induced voltage, judging by the way that they bundled the spark-plug wires together. Your engine will run better if you keep the wires separated at least ½-inch.

The Bendix starter drive is another source of consternation that you don't experience with a modern car. Here, the pinion gear is threaded on the drive. A shock loading spring is attached to the pinion gear. When the starter motor starts, the inertia of the gear and spring assembly causes the drive to screw the pinion gear into the flywheel gear. At this point, the starter is turning but the flywheel isn't. The shock spring winds up a little to give the flywheel time to get turning. When the engine starts, the flywheel gear overruns the pinion, causing it to screw away from the flywheel and disengage.

This Bendix drive has the left hand thread and spring. I must have robbed the bolt out of it.

Almost all car

engines turn clockwise. Looking from the front, therefore, the starter drive turns counter-clockwise. (A double-reduction starter motor will turn clockwise, but the drive turns the opposite direction.) Here is where the confusion comes: the Bendix spring needs to tighten the coils up as it engages the flywheel. If your starter is mounted

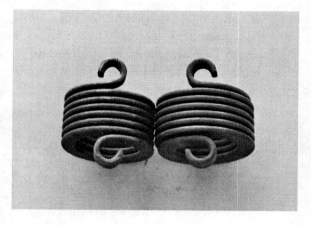

From left to right are a right hand Bendix spring and a left hand spring.

on the engine side of the flywheel and it pushes the pinion toward the flywheel, the Bendix drive will have right-hand threads. It is the same if the starter is on the right or left side of the engine. Look at the spring as a thread; it will also have a right-hand twist. When the starter drive is mounted outboard, it is pulled toward the flywheel. In this case, the Bendix drive will have a left-hand thread and a left wound spring. Now if this isn't confusing enough, some starters are mounted next to the transmission. Even though these will be clockwise starter motors, the drive will be counter-clockwise as viewed from the front of the engine. When the starter drive pinion moves toward the front of the car to engage the flywheel, it will have a left-hand thread and to the rear it will have a right-hand thread, regardless where the starter motor is mounted. The Bendix springs will be the same twist as the pinion thread.

I mention all of this because I have a bunch of Bendix springs that were used in the wrong application and are distorted out of shape. Somebody was putting them in wrong.

After the springs breaking in the Bendix drive, the bolts that hold them in place seem next on the failure list. These are called shoulder bolts and the shoulder should tighten up before the spring is tight under the head of the bolt. On the gear end of the Bendix, the thread of the bolt should not penetrate into the bore of the drive. The spring bolt on the drive end is usually used as a setscrew, locking it to the shaft. Before putting the drive assembly on the shaft, tighten the spring bolts. If you can see the thread end protruding into the bore, grind it off a bit. The bolts are locked in place with tab locks. These are about as rare as a 1943 steel penny. I have made some by using early Chevrolet V8 manifold bolt tab locks, but even they are getting hard to find. The best bet is to make some out of .030-inch mild steel. You bend one tab down into the eye of the spring and bend up the other tab on a flat of the bolt head after it is tight. A little Locktite on the threads won't hurt either.

I mentioned in the restoration section of this book that I didn't do much with the steering gear. This will not always be the case. If your restored car begins to wander on the road, it is time to check the steering components. A couple of simple tests will help locate the problem.

First, with the front wheel pointed straight ahead, turn the steering wheel to the right until it offers some resistance. Hold the wheel and put a mark on the steering column at the base of the steering wheel. Then turn the wheel to the left until resistance is felt. Look at your mark: if the wheel has moved up away from the mark, the thrust bearings on the worm are loose. These are adjustable by loosening a pinch bolt at the top of the steering gear and turning a collar in to tighten the bearings. Some steering gears use a bolt with a jam nut to push the collar in. There

This left hand spring was used in a right hand application. Notice the eyes are 180 degrees out of line and the coil is opened up.

should be no endplay and the steering wheel should stay in the same location in relation to the mark you made just below it.

Next, have someone turn the steering wheel left and right about ¼ turn. Watch the cross shaft — if it moves in and out as the wheel is turned, you will need to tighten the set screw on the backside of the steering gear. Turn it in until it pushes the cross-shaft tight inside the steering gear, then back off about ¼ turn. This should remove any endplay on the cross-shaft.

While checking for endplay, look and see if there is any bushing wear on the cross-shaft. The shaft will move fore and aft in relation to the steering gear. If this is the cause, you will have to replace the bushings and maybe turn the cross-shaft down to true it up.

If you still have excessive freeplay in your steering wheel, move the sector closer to the worm. You should jack the car up so both front wheels are off of the floor. Center the steering wheel and loosen all of the bolts that hold the cover to the steering gearbox. Usually on the top bolt there is an eccentric — turn it clockwise until the cover and cross shaft move closer to the worm. This should take maybe only ⅛ of a turn. Tighten the bolts back up and turn the steering wheel. There should be some drag in the center, but as the front wheels turn, the steering will free up in each direction.

When you tighten the setscrew on the cross shaft on a Ross steering gear, it moves the sector into the cam. This will take out the free travel.

But if after you have adjusted your steering gear but still can't get the free travel out of it, about the only option that you have left is to get it rebuilt.

If you have replaced the king pins and bushings when your car was restored, they should last almost forever, considering how collector cars are used. This wasn't the case when these old cars were daily drivers. Replacing the pins and bushings was a very common maintenance item. Today's vendors advertise them in some of the old car publications. Start with a publication that focuses on your make and model of car. If the vendor doesn't have the pins and bushings for your car, give him the measurements. Most medium-sized cars used

¾-inch diameter pins and the heavier cars used ⅞-inch pins. With the measurements, maybe he can find some that will work. Pins that are a little too long can be ground off. If the flat spot for the taper lock is in the wrong place, you can grind another.

When you have run out of other options, you can make pins for these. I have used drill rod, which can be bought at most any machine tool supply store. This is made of strong steel and precision-made enough for king pins. Drill rod is also machinable before it is heat-treated. I have made some king pins out of it where I had to drill and tap the ends where the grease covers are bolted to the pins. I had no trouble but be careful because it is tough steel and it would be easy to break a tap.

It is a simple task to make the bushings on a lathe. You can buy bushing stock at most bearing supply stores. It comes in 13-inch lengths, with a nominal inside and outside diameter. For instance, if you get ¾-inch by 1-inch bushing stock, that means it will be a little less than ¾-inch inside diameter and a little over 1-inch on the outside diameter.

If you are making bushings for ¾-inch pins, you can ream them to ¾-inch, then turn the outside about .010-inch oversized. When you press the bushings in place, this will shrink the inside diameter so you have some material to work with to get a tight slip fit. I have found this works and I don't need to ream the bushing after they are in place. There is not so much metal to remove that honing won't take care of it.

After the bushings are pressed in place, remove the grease fittings and drill a hole through the bushing so the grease can get in.

The thrust bearing for the spindle is usually a thrust ball bearing. I have never had trouble finding these at the bearing supply store. Ask for them by the bearing number, not the part number for your car. Put the open side down so water and dirt doesn't get into the bearing. If there is any vertical movement between the axle and spindle, shim under the thrust bearing.

The leaf springs in themselves aren't a source of trouble, but the shackle bolts are something that require attention. Take the leaf springs apart and sand off all the rust and grind out any notches that are wore into them from the shorter leaf below. On the end of the leaf that wears on the one above, grind a bevel on the end so that you don't have a sharp edge rubbing on the next leaf. This will remove the tendency for the springs to lock up.

After the springs have been painted, you can spread the leafs and squirt some grease between them with a needle on your grease gun. This can be done with the springs on the car — just take the weight off of them.

When I was young, the argument was in favor of not greasing your springs. There was some merit to this line of thought because of the dirt and gravel roads of that time. The grease made the grit stick to the springs, doing more harm than good. But with the kinds of roads an old car is driven on today, the grease sure will improve the ride and the grit won't be much of a problem.

The shackle bolts and bushings are a source of wear, though. The bushings can be made easy enough. You don't need the precision fit you require with the king pin bushings. I have bought some bushings at the hardware store and just ran a reamer through them after they were pressed into the spring eye. These hardware store bushings are too short, however, so get two for each spring eye if you should decide to go this route.

The original-looking shackle bolts are, of course, hard to find. I have bought new shackle bolts at the trailer and R.V. supplies outlet. By turning the heads to the shape of the original shackle bolts, I made a close resemblance to the original. Be sure to install the shackle bolts so that the grease groove is the opposite of the weight-bearing side of the bolt. You want the most wearing surface on where the weight is.

If you want to keep the original shackle bolts, you can build them up with weld and turn them true on a lathe. I wouldn't use brass to build them up, however, because it is always best to have dissimilar metals at a wear point.

The brakes are another component of the automobile that needs attention. In the days before self-adjusting brakes, this was a routine maintenance item. With mechanical brakes, you had rods or cables or both, to apply the brakes. When restoring a car, you will have to adjust these so that they apply the brakes on all four wheels equally. There are several ways to do this, depending on your make of car. I couldn't cover each procedure in detail, but the object is to have the brake cams in each wheel travel the same. Once you have the cables and rods set, you shouldn't need to adjust them again. As the brakes wear, just adjust the brake shoe to drum clearance.

All of the early cars that I have seen that were equipped with hydraulic brakes used Lockheed. (The Stutz, for a few years, used an expander-tube-type hydraulic brake similar to an aircraft brake.) Some Lockhead were an external band brake, as described in the brake section. Most were internal expanding shoe brakes.

Kantar Auto Parts sells brake parts for early Chrysler vehicles. Chrysler was the main user of Lockheed brakes. But even if your car isn't a Chrysler, it is a good chance they will have parts that will fit for your Lockheed brakes. It is important to get brand-new parts like brake hoses, since you don't want to use old original ones. Many of the cars used the same wheel cylinders, even though the master cylinder varied quite a bit. The most likely maintenance problem with hydraulic brakes is when the wheel cylinders leak. Honing out the cylinder and installing a new kit can easily fix that. If the cylinder is in bad condition, it will have to be sleeved to get a good surface or else it will still leak.

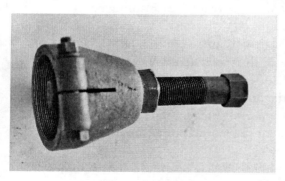

This is an old hub puller, which screws on where the hubcap goes. You then tighten the pinch-bolt and then screw the push-bolt in to force the axle out of the ehub.

With these Lockheed brakes, you will have to adjust the shoe anchor pin when you install new or relined brake shoes. Once this is done, you should only need to adjust the shoe to drum clearance. To do this, turn the eccentric anchor pin until it is farthest from the drum. Back off of the shoe adjuster as far as it will go. Then install the shoes and brake drum. Next, turn the rear anchor pin toward the rear of the car until the heel of the shoe has around .006-inch drum clearance. Turn the front anchor pin toward the front of the car to get the same clearance. Adjust the brakes for proper shoe-to-drum clearance. If your brakes drag a little in spots, don't worry about it. I have never seen a round-pressed steel brake drum.

The clutch is similar to the brakes in that once you get the linkage set, you only adjust the clutch for wear at the flywheel. The linkage should be set so that the throw-out bearing is in its travel range when the clutch pedal is in its travel range. With some clutches, the throw-out bearing pulls on the clutch levers; on others they are pushed in. With all the different setups, I can only generally discuss the linkage setup.

Most single disk clutches had a ring in the pressure plate to adjust the clutch for wear. The ring is locked in place with a spring pin or a tab fastened to the pressure plate. To adjust the clutch, unlock the ring, disengage the clutch and turn the ring clockwise to take up any wear. Lock the adjustor ring back in place and check the pedal for travel. You should have about 1 inch of free travel at the pedal after adjusting your clutch.

Some clutches had shims between the pressure plate and the flywheel. To adjust these, loosen the bolt and with a pair of needle-nose pliers and pull out a shim. (They are slotted and staggered for easy removal.) Tighten the bolt and turn the flywheel to the next one. Do the same until you have moved around the clutch. Don't take out more than one shim at a time, as they are difficult to get back in.

When doing maintenance on you collector car, you will find that new gaskets will be required. Of course, you can't just go to the auto parts store and buy one, so your next option is to make them.

For water connections like pumps, inlets and outlets use .020-inch to .030-inch thick paper. I like to use the thinnest paper possible because it puts less strain on the connection that you are bolting in place. Water outlets, like on a Model A Ford, are really susceptible to breakage due to the fact that the ears are weak and the outlet tends to warp. Model A mechanics that I have known file the outlets as flat as possible then they add an extra thickness of gasket to the outer edge of the ear. This way the bolt is less likely to bend the ear on the outlet down and break it off.

The best way to cut a gasket is to glue a piece of gasket paper to the removable part with contact-type gasket cement. Then using a small ballpeen hammer, tap around the object inside and out to cut the paper. For the boltholes, press around the gasket until you feel where the hole is, then tap over the hole with the ball end of the hammer and it will cut out the hole.

This method works well on gasket paper up to .030-inch thick. If you are making a gasket for something like a water pump, which has a raised shoulder or impeller, you will have to cut the center out first before gluing the gasket paper in place. Use a compass or find a round object that is the right size to draw around it. Cut out the center with a pair of scissors and check for fit before gluing it in place.

With thicker paper, about ¹⁄₁₆-inch thick, like with an oil pan gasket, then draw around the outside of the pan and mark all of the holes. With a gasket punch, cut the holes first. I like to use a piece of hard maple wood under the gasket when using the gasket punch. The wood is hard enough to back up the punch, but not so hard that it dulls it.

With scissors, cut on the line for the outside of the oil pans gasket. Using the holes as a guide; cut the inside of the gasket. Make sure to leave enough material between the bolt holes and the edge of the gasket. Leave the ends a little long and trim when you test it for fit.

On low pressure connections, like tappet or rocker arm covers, use cork gasket material, usually around ¹⁄₈-inch thick.

I like to glue all the gaskets in place with contact gasket cement on the part that is removable. On the other side of the gasket, use non-hardening Permatex or something similar. This way the gasket will come off when you remove a part and if you need to make a new one, you will have the pattern handy.

I feel that it is important to hold the gasket in place, especially during assembly. It doesn't do any good if it slips out of place.

In this section on maintenance, I have tried to cover the things that you don't deal with in a modern car. Some of the procedures could be considered a lost art, which is a good thing. These days nobody wants to work on their cars as often as people did when I was young. Now, these old cars are a hobby, so the maintenance is supposed to be fun and not work. So be sure that you enjoy yourself when you are working on your treasured automobile.

Chapter 13

Arizona To New York

I knew that they gave out awards to the people who drove their cars the longest distance to the annual Franklin Trek. I didn't have much hope of winning it because many of the Franklin Club members live in California, which would be farther from New York than I was. I was pretty new at the social aspect of the old car hobby and didn't realize how few owners actually drove their cars long distances.

In preparation for the trip, I had to make some changes on the car. I am too tall to fit in any car comfortably, let alone these older cars that were made when most people were smaller than they are now. My visibility looking out of the windshield on the Franklin was limited, especially trying to look up at the signal lights. My wife did not like it when she discovered that I watched the light reflections on the hood of the car to know when to stop and go.

My first attempt to alleviate this problem was to remove the outside sun visor, which gave me about two inches more of visible windshield. But to see up from inside the car, I had to slouch down. This would be acceptable for a short trip, but for a six-day cross-country drive, I needed to improve the situation.

This is when I went to Plan B: If I can't raise the car, I'll lower the driver. After removing the front seat cushion and looking it over, I concluded there wasn't much that I could do to improve it. So I decided to just make a replacement seat about three inches thinner. This would lower me down and hopefully improve my visibility.

I made a bed that would fit where the original cushion was

The Franklin is ready for the trip, except I haven't removed the hood side panels yet.

placed. I purchased some four-inch coil springs, which I covered with about two inches of padding. The seat cushion slopes to the rear, so I put more padding near the front edge and upholstered it like the original seat with the roll-type design.

Here again I got a bit too fancy. I should have used foam and done away with the springs. I didn't have enough padding over the springs and before the trip was finished, I could feel every one of them that I was sitting on. Needless to say, this made the trip very uncomfortable.

My new seat improved the visibility problem with some sacrifice to space for my legs. Changing your seat cushion isn't something most people will have to do, but unless you are challenging your endurance, it is best to start off as comfortable as possible.

The next thing that I felt needed to be done was to remove the hood side panels. During the Great American Race with my 1928 Dodge, we had trouble with vapor lock in the fuel system. After several attempts to solve the problem by insulating the gas line and putting a heat shield on the exhaust manifold, the trouble still persisted. Finally, we decided to remove the side panels, which solved our problem. An added bonus was that the car was much cooler inside because the engine heat was dissipated much faster.

I had never had a vapor lock problem with the Franklin, but being cooler inside appealed to me. After I had removed the panels, I made a padded box to put them in. The car looks better with them on, so I wanted to take them with me to New York. The box I made would just fit behind the front seat when I placed it on edge.

I figured that the car would suffer some paint chips and other minor damage you get from driving any car long enough. I didn't want to take a chance of breaking a headlight lens, since they are hard to find and those I could cost a minimum of $200.00 each. I solved that problem by making some padded headlight covers to fit over them, matched to the color of the car. Although I felt that it didn't help the appearance of the car, they weren't too bad and I could remove them when I got to the Trek.

Except for the routine maintenance, the car was ready to go. I filled the valve oiler and oiled the valve pads and checked the engine oil and gearboxes. I aired up the tires, including the spares, to 32 pounds of pressure. Then I drove over to the local station and filled the tank with gas. I wanted to be prepared in case of problems, so I took some tools and extra engine oil and put them in the trunk along with the jack and lug wrench. In the morning we would load up our personal effects and be ready for a real adventure.

My wife had two weeks off from her job and with the weekend, that would give us sixteen days to get to New York and back. I determined if we could travel 400 miles a day, then we would be there by the first day of the Franklin Club Annual Trek. With a map of the United States and a pair of dividers set for a distance of 400 miles, as per the map scale, I set out a route. I wanted to stay off of the freeways as much as possible but find towns large enough to have motels. This, by necessity, meant some variation in my 400-mile a day plan.

Day One was August 2, 2002. It was going to be hot in Wickenburg that day, so an early start was very important. I didn't see anyone in our neighborhood out and about so we slipped out of town undetected. Shirley and I drove north out of town seven miles on US Highway 93 until we came to the State Route 89 junction. This road took us up the Yarnell Hill, which gains around 2000 feet elevation in about 10 miles. I had driven the Franklin up this hill a dozen times with no problems, as long as I didn't lug the engine. We could run this car, and the one that I restored for the Great American Race, up this hill on a 110-degree day. If they didn't overheat here, then they would never overheat.

We continued north on SR-89 to Prescott where we stopped for coffee and a doughnut. Prescott is an old-car town with a good-sized car club. I had driven the Franklin up there several times, but still, not many of the residents had seen it. The stop for coffee was just prelude to the crowd that would gather every time we would stop on the rest of the trip.

Back on the road, we continued north on SR-89 to Ash Fork and then we turned east on I-40 to Flagstaff. I wanted to stay off of the freeway, but to get out of Arizona we did not have many options. At Flag (as the locals call it), we got gas and had breakfast. When we came out of the restaurant there was a crowd around our car. After talking old cars for about half an hour and telling them we were on our way to New York, we continued east on I-40. The freeway is fairly flat across northern Arizona, which was a good thing because of the 7000-foot elevation. I did open the main jet on the carburetor about one quarter turn to give it a little more gas. We cruised along about sixty miles per hour, but of course everyone else was doing eighty.

When we were near Gallup, New Mexico, we crossed the Continental Divide and so it was almost all downhill from there to the Mississippi River.

I tried to fix my gas gauge a couple of times, but it never did work with any consistency, so I couldn't depend on it. I decided to get gas every 200 miles, so that I would never take a chance of running out.

At Gallup, I filled the car with gas just as it started to rain. I got a little wet but it was no big deal. We got back on the freeway again and then it really started to rain. I was glad that I had put electric wipers on the car; they were getting a real workout. Keep in mind that they didn't work as well as on a modern car, but they were still better than the alternative, namely the old vacuum wipers. The clouds lowered until it was almost dark. I then jumped out of the car and removed my headlight covers, this time getting really wet. With the lights on and the wipers going, we proceeded down the highway at a somewhat slower pace.

The day was beginning to wear on me, but with just a little over 100 miles to go for the day, I was feeling good about our progress. The rain finally let up by the time that we reached Albuquerque, New Mexico, at about 5:00 in the evening. We got a room and some dinner and I decided to check the car over. I filled the valve oiler with oil and checked the valve lash; everything seemed to be in good order.

While I was fooling around with the car, I noticed quite a few other, older cars in the parking lot. Most of them were on trailers. I inquired of the owners of one who were nearby. They said that they were all going to the Reno car show. Their cars were from the 1950s and 1960s. They asked if I was going to Reno. "No," I replied. "We were on our way to New York." This seemed hard for them to accept: I was driving a 1930 car to New York, while they were hauling 1950s and 1960s cars to Reno. Of course, this was my first day on the road and I didn't know what lay ahead.

It had been a good day even with the rain. We had driven 487 miles in eleven hours since we had left home. I was over my goal of 400 miles a day, so I had some leeway in maintaining my average. I thought that this was going to be easy to keep with my schedule and even buy us some extra time.

On August 3rd, we were up at 5:00 in the morning. The car

was ready to go, except for gas. We like to drive for a while before we have breakfast, but there was not a good place to stop between Albuquerque and Tucumcari. Even though it was early, we ate some breakfast and then headed east on I-40. At each rest stop, we would get out and move around. I liked the Franklin because it was a bigger car than the others that I have had. But since I was 6'4" I was still cramped up.

At each stop, people would gather around trying to guess what kind of car it was. The only place its make is evident is on the hubcaps. The people asked a lot of questions and had stories of their own about an old car they had, or the ones of their fathers. It was as interesting listening to them as it was sharing what we were doing.

As we got near Tucumcari, we took a short stretch of the old Route 66, which leads up through the town. Here we took US-54, going northeast, through the corner of the Texas panhandle, then on across the Oklahoma panhandle. We stopped in Logan, New Mexico, for gas and a snack. Then we stopped once each in Texas and Oklahoma to get out and stretch and get a little exercise. This was a good road with very little traffic. It had been an uneventful day and the car was running great.

After we crossed into Kansas, we traveled the twenty miles to Liberal. Even though it was early, I had about all the enjoyment that I could stand for one day. It was hot and so all we ate were some melons and grapes. My wife wanted to check out the local Walmart, so we went shopping. Shopping isn't my thing, but walking around felt good.

On our second day on the road, we had traveled 385 miles in 10 hours. We stayed the night in Liberal and so I used up some of my extra miles from the day before. I was still on schedule.

The Franklin has an oil pump mounted on the firewall to oil the valves and the rocker arms. This is called a total-loss oiling system, because once the oil is used, it doesn't return. It tends to puddle up in a well around the valve springs, where it seeps out on the cylinder head. The cooling air blows it all over the firewall and the inside of the hood. With the hood side panel off, it got all over the right-side front fenders. I would use about a pint of oil a day, so by the second day, things were getting pretty messy. I cleaned up the oil the best that I could. The pump was putting out about the right amount that the manual said it should. It was good for about 400 miles per refill. Some of the oil was even getting on the right side of the windshield. I decided to not refill the pump and just oil the valve pads.

For this, I mixed up a concoction of Marvel Mystery Oil and STP. After removing the valve covers, I oiled the valves and rocker arm pivots. This seemed to be sufficient for the rest of the trip and it cut down on the oil mess considerably. I also leaned the carburetor back down to where it was before I opened the jet up, back near Flagstaff.

On August 4 we were up and ready to leave before daylight. We started north on US-83 to Sublette, Kansas. Even though I had cleaned up the oil mess, there was still a film on the windshield. At Sublette, we turned east on US-56 and the morning sun on the windshield made it almost impossible to see. We stopped at a service station and bought a bottle of window cleaner. After some effort with this cleaning, we were ready to leave and the windshield was much improved. As usual, even at this early hour, people gathered around asking questions, even when I just stopped to clean the windshield. It took at least half an hour to get going again. When people show an interest in the car, I didn't want to be rude and just leave. Besides, this is a big part of the fun of driving it.

US-56 brought us up to Dodge City, where we had breakfast. The wife spotted an art show and being an artist herself, we had to take a look at the artwork. After a couple of hours, it was time to get out of Dodge. We were back on US-56 going northeast toward Great Bend. The map shows that this is a scenic route, but what we remember of this scenic route was the smell of the stockyards. I am sure that to the local people it smells like money, but to us it smelled like what it was.

It was getting hot and the wind kicked up. It felt like it was blowing about twenty or thirty miles an hour from the south. Every time a gust of wind would hit the car broadside, it wanted to head downwind. I may have put too much caster in the front axle. The car drove well most of the time, but with a crosswind and rutted roads, I had to keep a good grip on the steering wheel.

At Great Bend we got gas and lunch. My plan to make 400 miles today would take us out of Kansas, so we were anxious to get going. A few miles out of Great Bend we got on SR-156, which led us to I-70. This was the first time that we were back on a freeway since we had left I-40 near Tucumcari, New Mexico. We went due east on I-70 for twenty-six miles until we came to the US-81 junction. We turned north on US-81. Shirley and I were both feeling totally fatigued. She thought it was due to the heat and dehydration. We stopped at a convenience store and bought some juice and water. After resting for a while and drinking some fluids we began to feel much better. I think it was about this time that I figured out why people don't drive old cars across the country.

We were back in the car again and we continued north on US-81 until we reached US-36. We then turned east and I felt somewhat refreshed, even though it had been the most trying day so far. It was also the shortest day, in miles, that we had covered. I checked the map and the next town that looked big enough to have some motels was Marysville. We got there about 4:00 in the afternoon. The next stop would be St. Joseph, Missouri, and I didn't feel I could make it that far. After getting a room, we walked across the highway to the pizza place. There is nothing like a pizza and beer to make you feel better. I decided to get the car ready for the next morning. I oiled the valve pads and checked the valve lash. With just a slight adjustment on a couple of exhaust valves, everything was in good shape. A couple of guys came over as I was fooling around the car. One of them was telling me he had an old pickup truck he intended to restore, but just never got around to it. I tried to encourage him to get started on it. I believe it was then that I got the idea to write a book on restoring a car. People think that it is a daunting task, but if you break it down to several simple tasks, it won't be as intimidating.

This was Day Three of the trip and we had only covered 371 miles. My average was still over 400, but I wanted to get the extra miles during the western part of our journey. With the possibility of car trouble, I could not afford to lose too much time and still be at the Trek on the first day. But as a matter of fact, the car was holding up better than I was.

August 5th and another early start before daylight. It is a good thing that we are early risers. The first thing I needed to do was to get gas for the car and coffee for us. While filling the car with gas, a guy noticed the Arizona license plate and asked if we had drove the car from Arizona. He didn't believe it when I said yes. "You must have hauled it," was his reply. It made me think why ask a question if you don't want to hear the answer. My next thought was that maybe I appeared to him to be smart enough not to drive an old car that far. Well, smart or not, we were back on the US-36 going east. I am glad I didn't tell him where we were going and the fact we were only about halfway there. It wasn't very many miles to St. Joseph, Missouri, where we planned to have breakfast. But by the time I got through the traffic congestion, I was out of the town and hadn't seen one good place to eat.

US-36 turned into a four-lane road, smooth and straight, so we cruised along about sixty miles an hour. I noticed a truck stop in Cameron, so we pulled in for breakfast. It was good food, even though my wife thought it looked like a truck stop, which in fact it was.

We continued east, straight across Missouri. This was uneventful except for a gas stop at Mooresville. This, of course, brought a crowd to look at the car. It was becoming routine but I always took time to visit with the people. After all, they seemed sincerely interested in the car and what we were doing. At Hannibal, Missouri, we took some time to look the town over. This is where Mark Twain grew up so it is quite a tourist attraction. It was really hot and humid, but to get out and walk around felt good. After finding a little place where we got a big glass of ice tea, I was feeling somewhat refreshed.

The Franklin parked on a side street in Hannibal, Missouri. Note that the hood side panels are off. It was around 103 degrees this day with not many people out and about.

We were back in the car again. We crossed the Mississippi River and then turned north on I-172. We drove toward Quincy, Illinois, until we came to US-24. We were supposed to turn on US-136, but I missed the turn because the junction wasn't very well-marked. The next town we came to was Lewiston, Illinois. I checked my map and discovered that I wasn't supposed to be there. It was a little town really off of the beaten path. When we stopped at a convenience store to ask directions and to get something to drink, a crowd of people circled the car. Shirley was able to get out, but people were standing so close to my side I couldn't get my door open. I asked what was the best way to get back on US-136. We heard several responses, all the way from "you can't get there from here," to "take the road in front of the store south and it will intersect US-136." That last one sounded like the best bet, so that is what we did. Shirley finally came back out of the store and was talking to all of the people, too. She really hated to leave, since everyone there was so friendly. Even though we were getting used to a crowd gathering when we stopped, I still couldn't get over how many showed up so fast. Everyone wanted to help and wanted to know where we were going and a dozen other questions. These people had a special feel about them and we've always considered this one of the high points of our trip.

After spending about forty-five minutes in Lewiston, we went south on what turned out to be SR-78 along the Illinois River. We turned left on US-136 and were going east again. The road was straight and in good condition, but it seemed like there was a little town every five to ten miles. I decided maybe the freeway wasn't such a bad idea after all. I was driving fifty-five or sixty miles an hour where I could, but I still had traffic backed up behind me most of the time. This was beginning to make me a bit nervous. On these two lane roads, cars couldn't, or wouldn't, pass. Every time I would get up to speed, I would come to another little town. About halfway across Illinois we came to Heyworth, at the junction of I-55.

We checked in at a motel and met the crabbiest motel clerk ever. She had a personality like a wounded coyote. She definitely needed an attitude adjustment. What a contrast to the people we had met earlier in Lewiston, just about 100 miles to the west!

This was Day Four and we had driven 434 miles in 12 hours since we had left Marysville. We had taken a short tour of Hannibal, Missouri, got lost, but met some great people. I was really tired, but all-in-all it was a good day.

August 6th: I woke up this morning and felt more tired than when I went to bed. I didn't sleep too well, but then I never do in a motel. I considered turning back, but Shirley convinced me to finish the trip. I always finish what I start, so after a few cups of coffee, I felt somewhat revived.

Yesterday had been spent going through dozens of little farm towns and I was ready to try the freeways again. I-55 ran right past the motel, so I checked the map and found if I took it north and then turned east on I-80, I would miss Chicago, which I surely wanted to avoid. The problem was that I would have to go through

Gary, Indiana, to be able to eventually get to the Turnpike. So far I had managed to miss any big cities. I thought that going through just this one couldn't be too bad.

I oiled the valve pad with my mixture of Marvel Mystery Oil and STP. This seemed to work and I didn't have oil spreading every-where like I was experiencing with the valve oiler. At a near-by station I put in 22 gallons of gas. I had lost track of where I had last got gas, but it was a lot farther than the 200 miles that I had planned on. The original gas tank held twenty gallons but while I was restoring the car, I had a larger twenty-four gallon tank made. This was the first time that I needed the extra capacity, which was a good thing considering I hadn't been paying attention like I should have been.

With everything back in the car, we hit the road again, going north on I-55 through Bloomington, Indiana. Shirley thought she smelled gas, so I got off of the freeway and checked the car over. I didn't find anything wrong; maybe I had filled the tank too much and some of the gas overflowed. On the freeway again, we cruised along at about sixty, and I began to relax and feel more confident again. We were getting hungry and started watching for a place to eat.

At Chenoa, we spotted a place that looked good: a nice restaurant right on the old Route 66 that the locals appeared to frequent. We pulled up in front of the building where you could see the car from inside. By the time we were out of the car, a crowd had gathered. I took time to show them the car and answer their questions. About half-an-hour later, we finally got inside the restaurant and I was really hungry by then. Our waitress took our orders, took them to the kitchen, and then sat in the booth with us. She asked a lot of questions and told about an old car she had. We were wondering when breakfast was going to be served when Shirley noticed that the cook and the other kitchen help had come around the outside corner of the building and were out looking at the car. Some of the local farmers told us about old cars they had in the past, but none had any now. This is a good way to find old cars in barns, but it wasn't to be on this day.

We finally got our breakfast and were very glad for it. It was one-and-a-half-hours before we were ready to leave. You don't want to be in a hurry when driving an old car that attracts this much attention. This is a good time to slow down and smell the flowers along the way.

The car was running fine; we had a full stomach and were cruising along smoothly. Things were going great. Then we made a right turn on to I-80 for the drive through Gary, Indiana. Right away there was a whole lot more traffic. Trucks were passing on both sides of us and the road got really rough and the lanes appeared to be narrower. I tried to stay in the right lane, but more lanes were added every few miles until I-80 was six lanes wide! Everyone but me was going at least seventy-five miles an hour. Wind from the passing trucks blew the Franklin around and the pavement was as rough as a creek bottom. Also, because we had no air conditioning and had the windows open to get what air we could, the wind noise was terribly nerve-wracking. This was a white-knuckle experience if there ever was one.

After enduring about as much as I could stand, the exit for the turnpike appeared on the overhead sign. Three more miles and we bailed off of the freeway to the tollbooth. I have heard of life in the fast lane, but a half-hour of it must have aged me five years. After what we had just been through, the turnpike was better than a paid vacation. Cars and trucks still passed, but only on the left side and there weren't many of them. There were rest stops every thirty or forty miles with gas and food. Their access lanes were well marked and the stops were easy to enter and exit.

This was the best driving of the whole trip. We would stop at about every other rest stop. People came up and asked about the car, as before. They said that they had just passed us a few miles back and couldn't guess what type of car it was. After explaining and walking around some to limber up, we would be back on the road. We stopped and ate lunch just after crossing into Ohio. We were making good mileage and the distance we had yet to go looked to be an easy goal, so we stopped early near Fremont, Ohio.

The motel had a pool and a bar and we took time to relax the rest of the day and evening. When I checked the map, I saw the only place I would have to get off of the turnpike was Cleveland. We had stopped there when I did the Great American Race; no way would we have stayed there again, even if we had to drive late into the night.

This had been Day Five of our trip and we had covered only 369 miles, but with two days to go, it would be easy driving to get to Syracuse, New York.

This was August 7th. We had had a restful night's sleep. I was eager to get started. I went through my routine of checking the car over; we loaded everything back up and got back on the turnpike. After about eighty miles, we had breakfast at one of the rest stops. I didn't want to go through Cleveland, especially after the experience of driving through Gary, so we stayed on the turnpike south of Cleveland to Interstate 271. This freeway went north to the I-90 junction. Here we turned east and traveled along with very little traffic. At SR-534, we went north to a state park called Geneva-on-the-Lake. After spending some time at the lake, we got back in the car and on the road again. We went east on SR-531 until we reached the Pennsylvania border. Here, we got back onto the freeway and continued to Buffalo, New York. I could have stayed on I-90 and made it easy to Syracuse this day but we had time and had never been in this part of the country. We decided to take in some of the sights that were available.

At Buffalo, we crossed into Canada. The border guard talked with us for a long time as cars continued to line up behind us. He was interested about our trip from Arizona. He told us to take the parkway down the Niagara River to the falls. It was a beautiful and relaxing drive. After spending some time at the falls, we decided to get a room on the Canadian side. It was so much more peaceful and calm, even though it was bustling with people from all over the world. We checked out the hotels and found only one with a room left. Needless to say we grabbed it up: $250.00 for one night. This is the cost of not planning ahead. It was 5:00 in the evening and I was ready to call it a day. Shirley loved the room. I have noticed through the years, her love for a room is in direct proportion to the cost. It was a great room with a balcony and a big red heart shaped Jacuzzi tub. After this long drive, Shirley got $250.00 worth from just the Jacuzzi alone.

I went down to the car to get some of our luggage. While there, I decided to check the valve lash again and oil the valve pads. By the time I had finished, a crowd had gathered, so I spent an hour or more answering all of their questions. I had a scrapbook of the restoration and some of them looked through it. I don't know how many I inspired to get started on their own restoration projects. Some of them, after seeing my before pictures, thought their project wouldn't be too difficult.

This was Day Six: We had driven about 357 miles in about eleven hours since we had left the motel near Fremont, Ohio. We spent some time at the state park and quite awhile at Niagara Falls. It was nature at its breathtaking best. Shirley got in a little tourist shopping and enjoyed the relaxation in the Jacuzzi. This stop gave her some time to do the girl things. With less than 200 miles left to travel, the end was in sight.

The next day was Thursday, August 8th. We didn't need to check in at the Franklin Trek until Friday. The car was giving us no trouble at all. We decided that we weren't in any big hurry to get there. After coming this far, we thought we might as well see some of the sights. After crossing back into the United States just north of the falls, we took SR-18 to the old Fort Niagara. It was fascinating.

We spent several hours there and then proceeded along the lakeshore on SR-18. We had still not had anything to eat yet today, and we were really getting hungry, when we came to a resort area. Here we had a leisurely meal. It was a really nice place and we were in no hurry to get going again. We then drove along the lake for quite awhile. I turned south on SR-98 and stopped for some gas at a convenience store. This was the first time that nobody paid any attention to the car, even though there were a lot of people coming and going from the store. I thought that maybe people were used to seeing Franklins so it wasn't a big deal to them. At least it didn't take long to get gas and back on the road. After about twenty-six miles on SR-98 we turned onto I-90 again. It wasn't very far to Syracuse. As we drove through the city, we saw a sign to Cazenovia, which is where the trek would be and where we had a motel reservation.

After taking the exit toward Cazenovia, we never saw another sign. It was supposed to only be about twenty miles to our destination, so I just went south and east as the roads took us. The problem was, this was hill country and the roads would wind around until I didn't know where I was.

As a last resort, and at Shirley's urging, I stopped and asked directions. Or more correctly, I sent Shirley into a little store to ask. After a bit, though, I followed her in. The person behind the counter said that we couldn't get there from here. I had heard that one before in Lewiston, Illinois. Then a customer came in and explained how to get to Cazenovia. He knew the country well; following his directions, we took four different roads, some state and some country. Sure enough, we came into Cazenovia on SR-13 from the north.

This was our destination. After a week on the road, I could finally really relax. The car had given us no trouble at all; you might say it was a hell of a test drive. The driver, however, didn't hold up as well, what with the August heat, the wind noise due to having the windows down, and the traffic. I was exhausted. But the sum of all the good we had added up to a great experience.

This had been Day Seven on the road and we had covered 221 miles in about ten hours. After checking into the motel, we walked to a nearby restaurant and had dinner. That night I went to sleep, feeling good that I had accomplished this task. I had restored a car that was ready for the grave, and with some trial and error, I had made it dependable enough to drive it across the country.

August 9th was the first day of the Franklin Club's Annual Trek. We couldn't check in until around 10:00 a.m. We found a car wash and a Laundromat right next to each other. I cleaned the car and put the hood side panels back on. Shirley did the laundry, and between the two of us we used about $10.00 worth of quarters. After returning to the motel and unloading the rest of the stuff out of the car, we were ready to check in to the event.

CHAPTER 14

The Franklin Club Trek

The Franklin automobile was never made in great numbers, but the people that own them are devoted to the marque.

In 1951, a few owners and fans got together and formed the H.H. Franklin club, one of the earliest car clubs. The meetings were held in Syracuse and were called the "Franklin Trek." The club grew and, in 1970, the Trek was moved to Cazenovia, about twenty miles from Syracuse. It has been held at the Cazenovia College ever since. The club now has between 800 to 900 members. About half of them turn out at the Trek each year. Some attendees are second and third generation Trekkers.

The 2002 Trek was a special one, in that it was held in conjunction with the City of Syracuse, where the cars were produced, and the centennial celebration of Franklin History. Because of this, the trek was nine days instead of the usual seven days as other years.

If you were a first timer at the Trek, you had nametags that were a different color than the ones the old-times had. Judging from these, about 60 percent of the members were there for the first time. I am not sure of the figure, but a lot of the people had nametags that were the same color as ours.

There were things to do each day, like arts and crafts for the women, club sales and swap meet, etc. People were free to participate or not. The thing that most interested me was the short trips in the Franklins. Some people didn't have a car, but they could get a ride with the people that did. We could only spend three days there, because of my wife's schedule, but we tried to make the most of our time.

We parked our Franklin along with the others at the Cazenovia College.

After asking directions to the college, we arrived about 10:00 in the morning. We had pre-registered before leaving home, but still had to check in. While checking in, they asked if we brought a car. "Yes. In fact we drove it," was my reply. They looked at us amazed or disbelieving. I am not sure which. They told us we could stay in the dorms at the college, but after looking at the small beds, I knew that I could not fit in any of them; therefore, we decided to stay at the motel.

We parked the car on the grass with the other fifty or sixty Franklins that were already there. We walked around looking at the cars for an hour or so. More cars were beginning to arrive. I was thinking about what more I could do with my Franklin. I have shown it locally, made several short trips, drove it across country and now I've brought it to a national meet. After talking to Shirley, I decided this would be a good place to sell the car. Where else would

The new owner, Lloyd Wilson, with the car at the college.

you find so many Franklin enthusiasts? I put a "FOR SALE" sign in the window. By this time lunch was being served and we were ready to eat.

While we were eating lunch in the college cafeteria, one of the new club members, whose name was Lloyd Wilson, sat down at our table. There was no chitchat: He just got right to the point: "I think that you are the man that I want to see. It is your car that is for sale?"

"Yes," I said.

"I'll take it," he said as he was getting out his checkbook.

"Don't you want to look it over," I asked.

"I looked it over before I came in for lunch. They tell me that you drove it here from Arizona, so it must be a good car. The only problem is that my wife and I flew up here from South Carolina, and we have to fly back on Monday."

"There must be someplace in Syracuse that could have the car shipped for you," was my reply.

"Could you drive it to South Carolina?" he asked.

I wasn't too keen on the idea of driving it all the way down there, but before I could answer, my dear wife spoke up and said yes, we could. Later she explained that a two-day drive to South Carolina was better than a six-day drive back home. She seemed to disregard the fact that the car had only been for sale for about thirty minutes. At any rate, we made the deal and the couple that bought the car rode with us the next two days on the short drives around the area. This way the buyer got the opportunity to see how well the Franklin would perform.

This was a day to get acquainted with everyone and get a look at all the other cars. The club was expecting more Franklins at this Trek than ever before and they weren't disappointed. More of them kept arriving all day. I ran into a couple of guys that I had met at a

This was taken during a short trip to the windmills near Cazenovia, New York.

Wickenburg barbeque. I was surprised to meet people I knew so far from home.

On Saturday, August 10th, there were several events going on. There was a technical session, workshops, etc. As for me, I took the short driving tours of some nearby towns and a lunch on the road. You would think that I would have had enough of driving and eating on the road, but this was different: we didn't travel that far and we were in the company of other Franklin owners and drivers. I never gave a thought of having to get in my 400-miles-a-day.

Sunday, August 11th, was the big day for the Franklin Centennial. We went to the college that morning and had breakfast. Around 9:00 a.m. all of the people that wanted to drive their Franklins to Syracuse left the college. We proceeded to the Drumlins Country Club and parked our cars in order of the year of manufacture, for the Syracuse event. With a police escort, we left the Country Club with the oldest cars first. Our destination was the downtown square in Syracuse. After parking the cars on the street, I tried to get a picture of every car. With the crowds of people around it was difficult to get pictures at all. I got some individually, but most of the time it was three to four cars to a picture.

Some estimate that there were 165 Franklins there that day. Even though some owners hauled their cars close to the downtown square and only drove them the last few miles, most drove their cars from Cazenovia.

There was a lot going on in Syracuse that day, but I spent most of the time talking to the other club members. We had lunch in a big tent set up for that purpose. I also took in the museum, near the downtown square. They had the first Franklin ever sold, and by some accounts, the third one made.

Around 3:00 in the afternoon, all of the Franklins started back to Cazenovia. We were on our own as far as directions went. I didn't know my way around, so I followed a couple of the other Franklins. They didn't know their way either, but after asking directions we all got on the right road. Several cars had problems on the way back, but our car ran just fine.

There were an estimated 165 Franklins in Syracuse on August 11, 2002.

There were more events at the college that evening, including a wine and cheese party. This was our last day, since we had to deliver the car to South Carolina and be home within a week. I wish that we could have stayed longer as I was getting to know a few people. There were events planned for the next week, some of which seemed like they would be very interesting. But after getting back to the motel from the college, we packed some of our things in the car in preparation to leave.

On Monday, August 12th, we got up early before daylight and loaded the rest of our personal gear into the car. It was about 800 miles to South Carolina, so I reverted back to my 400-miles-per-day plan. I decided not to remove the hood side panels for just a two-day trip. I did save the storage box for them, just in case it got too hot in the car.

We started west on US 20, which seemed like the wrong direction, but it was the shortest route to Interstate 81. We turned south on I-81 and we were now headed toward our destination. The car was purring like a kitten and I had gotten some rest during the Trek, so I wasn't as tired as when we arrived.

The only problem now was the fog. The old Franklin headlights, even though they were twelve inches in diameter, weren't very bright. I did replace the original six-volt, thirty-candlepower bulbs with twelve-volt, fifty-candlepower bulbs. This may have aggravated the problem. As anyone who has driven in the fog knows, when your lights are on high beam, the light reflects off the fog and reduces visibility. Good fog lights are mounted close to the road with a yellow-tinted lens. The high-mounted Franklin lights weren't providing much visibility, even on low beam. The only other choice I had was to drive slower and keep a close lookout ahead. Then I worried if going too slow would cause someone to rear-end me, as the taillights aren't the brightest either. Finally daylight came and soon the fog dissipated. We had dodged another possible misfortune. I was more concerned than ever of getting the car delivered in one piece. If it was my car, I would have dealt with any problem, but now I didn't own the car and I could just imagine the ramifications of a mishap.

This is why I didn't want to deliver the car in the first place. Unfortunately, my wife thinks that I can do anything with no problem.

Near the Pennsylvania border we stopped for breakfast. The day was overcast, but getting warmer. We continued south on I-81 through the hills of Pennsylvania. Everything was going well. As I drove along, I began to wonder if maybe I shouldn't have sold the car. After the arduous trip of getting to the Trek, maybe I hadn't used good judgment. Oh well, life moves on and I did get several leads on other cars that needed restoration.

I didn't spend too much time visiting with the people when we stopped for gas or something to drink. I just wanted to get the car delivered before something happened.

We crossed the narrow portions of Maryland and West Virginia. As the day wore on, it was getting hotter and more humid. The car was much warmer inside, because the side panels of the hood were still on. I felt if we could just endure it, we could make it.

Somewhere in Virginia the engine just stopped running. I had never had a vapor lock problem the whole time driving through Arizona, which was hotter than it was on this day. I first checked the ignition. The coil felt warmer than it should have, which indicated the points were closing up. (The longer the points are closed, the more current goes through the coil.) Luckily, the freeway had a wide shoulder where we stopped so I could get well away from the traffic. Unfortunately, I opened the door and stepped out on a big wad of chewing gum, which about glued me to the road. After a futile attempt to clean off my shoe on the guardrail, I just went ahead and adjusted the ignition points by the eyeball method. The car started up and ran fine, so we were back on the road again. After about five miles, the car started to cut out but kept running. We took the next exit from the freeway, which led us to some restaurants and other tourist stops.

Shirley said that we needed to take off the hood side panels. I know she doesn't know much, if anything, about mechanical things, but it wouldn't hurt. At least the car would be cooler inside. We drove to a restaurant and had lunch. I ordered a salad and some fruit, but couldn't eat much. I guess I never got rested as much as I thought at the Trek, plus the day was really hot and humid. It is hot in Arizona, but that is a dry heat.

We had to unload the car to get to the box for the side panels. Then I put the panels in the box and loaded everything back in the car. This didn't take too long. I then rechecked the points. We were ready to head south again. With the hood side panels off of the car, it wasn't quite as hot inside and the engine never missed a beat the rest of the trip. Shirley still claims that it was her idea that fixed the problem. I have my doubts, but it is hard to argue with success.

After another hour of driving, it was time to get gas and something to drink. I came to one of those roundabout-type exits that were under construction. I had no problem finding a station with a convenienence store. After getting gas and walking around a little, we got back into the car. The signs were down due to the construction, but I took the obvious road to enter the freeway. In all the years my wife and I have traveled, she always asks if I am going the right way when we enter the freeway. She has no sense of direction and gets turned around very easily. Well, this time she never said a word. That in itself should have clued me in. We were back on the freeway, but after a short time it seemed to me we were going in the wrong direction, but with all of the loops and curves it took to get onto the freeway, I wasn't sure. After a couple of miles the milepost numbers were getting bigger while I was sure that they should be getting smaller. Finally, the sun broke through the overcast and sure enough, it was on the wrong side of the car. By this time, I had gone ten miles north and it was another ten miles before I could find an exit to turn around. The first and only time I had ever gone the wrong way. You might say I was losing my mental focus; at least I wasn't ready to take the Mensa test.

I had gone twenty miles north, then I had to go back that twenty miles south over again. I kept thinking where we could have been if I had those forty miles back. My mental lapse was confirmed when I discovered, that evening, that I also had forgotten to put the gas cap back on the last time we stopped for gas.

We finally reached the interchange where I-64 intersected with I-81. We came to an exit that was marked as having motels. After checking in and resting awhile, I checked our progress. We had traveled 504 miles, plus the forty miles of extra adventure we enjoyed that day. This had been the longest day's drive since we had left Arizona. With only about 300 miles to go tomorrow, I figured that would be an easy day.

I checked the car over as I routinely did: oiling the valve pads and adding some engine oil. I also figured out why the engine cut out: The resistor for the coil had come loose and would pivot around the one bolt that held it in place. In some positions it would short out until the bolt finally came out. Then it just hung on the electric wires, but clear of anything that would cause it to short out. I didn't have another bolt with me, but it had been running okay, so I decided to just let it be for now.

It was now Tuesday, August 13th. We got an early start as usual. I was anxious to get going. With some luck, this would be the last day. I filled the car with gas and looked around for where I could buy a gas cap. There was nothing open but some gas stations and they don't carry parts anymore. I rolled up a sock and stuffed it into the filler neck to keep the gas from slopping out.

We got back on I-81 going south and we cruised along about sixty miles per hour. The car was running great and I felt it was just a matter of time before we would be at our destination. I started feeling a little sad that the car and I would be parting company soon. We have been through a lot this last week (or nine days to be exact). Still, I had to remind myself, we possess things but cannot let things possess us.

About this time the engine noise seemed to get louder. I came to an exit that didn't have much there but a truck stop. I checked the engine over and discovered a stud that holds the exhaust pipe to the manifold had come out. I also discovered that I had forgotten to put the oil filler cap back on. I got to thinking that between the parts that I was losing and the bolts that were falling off, there wouldn't be anything left to deliver if we drove far enough.

I didn't think that I could find a stud, nut and washer here, so I looked for a ⁷⁄₁₆-inch bolt. A guy at the truck stop couldn't (or wouldn't) help me out. About this time I saw a mechanic's truck drive up. Having been a field mechanic myself, I was sure he would have something that would work. Also, being a mechanic, he might be willing to help.

I was right on both counts! He dug around and found a 1½-inch by ⁷⁄₁₆-inch bolt in his bucket.

"You will need a lock washer and a flat washer also, won't you?" he asked.

"I could use a lock washer but there is not enough clearance for the flat washer," I replied. I offered to pay him, but he wouldn't take anything.

I tightened up the exhaust and we were ready to get going again. The car sounded normal, so I pointed it south and away we went. After awhile we stopped for breakfast, and then we got back on the road. I-81 began to head in a more westerly direction, so in order to go south, we took I-77. At this point, it was only around twenty miles to the North Carolina border. Just one more state to cross and we would be in South Carolina.

Our trip through North Carolina was uneventful, which of course, is what we wanted. North of Charlotte, we stopped to get something to drink and to get refreshed. The day was getting hotter and hotter and even more humid. Not knowing what to expect going through the city, I wanted to be as alert as possible. As it turned out, that didn't become much of a problem. When we came to the interchange of I-77 and I-85, I took a right turn. The traffic wasn't too heavy and the exit was well-marked. Now, all we had to do was stay on I-85. This was the last leg of the journey. About twenty miles past Charlotte we came to the South Carolina border.

With less than a hundred miles to go, the end was in sight. The car was performing well and I felt somewhat revived, even though it was getting hotter. At about fifty miles from our exit, we stopped again for some refreshments and walked around to limber up. We got back in the car feeling really good and the miles seemed to go by quite quickly. The next thing we knew we were approaching our exit. Shirley got out the directions to the new owner's home. We had no problem finding it. I missed one street, but since there was no traffic, I just backed up and made the turn.

At around 3:00 in the afternoon the car was delivered, except for the parts I lost. The owner said he didn't expect us that early; in fact, he was worried whether we would make it.

As it turned out, he wasn't the only one that didn't think that we would. Back at the Trek in New York, some of the members of the Franklin Club didn't think that we would either. I got the feeling that they didn't believe that we drove that 1930 Franklin from Arizona to the Trek and then drive it another 800 miles to South Carolina. That was more than they could fathom. The owner sent an e-mail back to the Trek, telling them that we had arrived, I guess to prove that we had made it by Tuesday afternoon after all.

In nine days of driving, we had covered 3,494 miles, not counting the 40 miles I had lost going the wrong way and also the trips taken at the trek. The car held up really well, except for the minor incidents that I have mentioned. The driver didn't do as well some of the time, but a good meal and a night's sleep did wonders to fix that.

I never heard from the Franklin Club about who drove their car the farthest to the Trek, but some of the members were sure we were the ones. It is not important to me to be recognized for something; after all, we had an experience that I will never forget and that's what is most important. But should any of the members that were there read this book, maybe this will put their doubts to rest.

Wednesday, Aug 14th: We have left the great hospitality of the Franklin's new owner. He had treated us with the great Southern hospitality you always hear about. We had a great dinner at an especially nice restaurant. The bed that we slept in beat any motel beds anywhere across the country: we slept the best we had in many a night. We rented a car, loaded our stuff and headed back west to Arizona, arriving home with a day to spare.

What an experience the last two weeks had been! This had

The new owners of the Franklin, Lloyd and Jane Wilson, at their home in South Carolina. Notice that we cleaned the car and replaced the hood side panels.

closed a chapter in our lives. We had taken the old Franklin through all the phases, from the restoration to car shows, a cross-country trip, a national club meet, where we jointed the centennial celebration of the Franklin company and then finally passed it on to a new owner. After getting home, I decided all that was left was to put it all into book form. I still miss the Franklin sometimes, but it is time to move on. Who knows, I may find another car in my wanderings, one that I just can't pass up and I will be able to start up another relationship.

Index